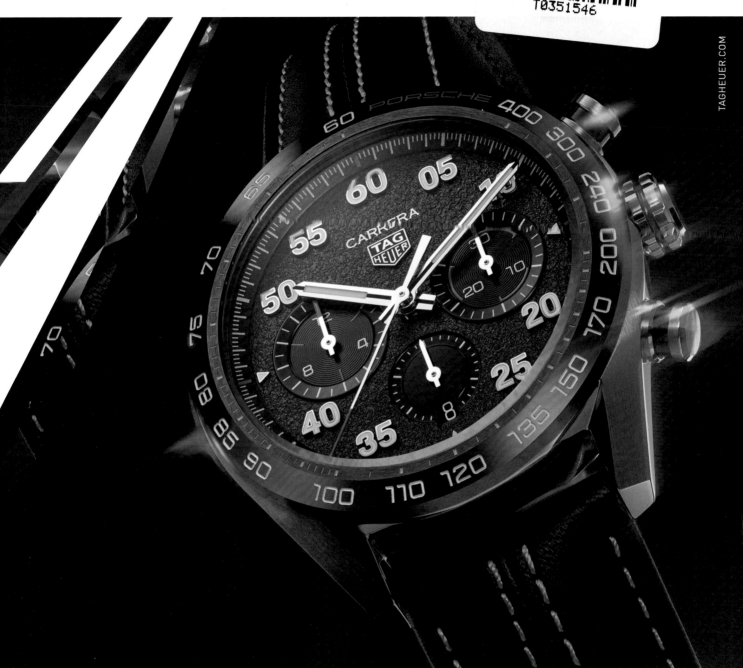

TAGHEUER.COM

 ×

TROLLSTIGEN

INTRO

Norwegen. Das Land im Westen Skandinaviens übt auf viele eine magische Anziehungskraft aus. Diese CURVES-Ausgabe fährt mitten hinein, in majestätische Naturwunder und Geheimnisse. Will nachsehen und zeigen, wie Norwegen wirklich ist. Und wir sind ausgesprochen zuversichtlich, dass uns genau das gelungen ist: die fremdartige, berührende Schönheit der Fjorde und Gebirge einzufangen und gleichzeitig auch die bestürzende Weite aufzuzeigen. Trotzdem soll hiermit eine kleine Gebrauchsanweisung für CURVES Norwegen gereicht werden: Gehen Sie nicht davon aus, dass die spektakulären Szenen der Reise leicht zugänglich zu erfahren sind oder geballt auftreten. Auch die langen Geraden und hartnäckig erkämpften Meilen zwischen den Sensationen gehören zu Norwegen. Es ist ein Land für Fortgeschrittene. Fernweh und die Suche nach purer Fahrfreude, das Unterwegssein im CURVES-Rhythmus, finden hier tiefe Befriedigung. Übrigens: Als Fahrende, die in Sportwagen-Kategorien denken, stellen wir eines fest: Hier in Norwegen ist es immer noch nur das Automobil, diese magische Freiheitsmaschine, die uns zu den schönsten Winkeln bringt. Norwegen ist so enorm groß, dass ohne ein Auto nahezu überhaupt nichts geht. Fahrradfahrer sollten unfassbar lange Beine haben, um vorwärtszukommen, und Motorradfahrer einen Hintern aus Eisen. Egal, wie Sie die Reise angehen: Erleben Sie nun mit uns – Norwegen. *Soulful Driving.*

—

Norway. This western outpost of Scandinavia holds a magical attraction for many people. This issue of CURVES drives straight to the heart of the country's majestic natural wonders and mysteries. Our stated aim is to find out what Norway is really like. We're extremely confident that we've succeeded in doing just that: capturing the strangely moving beauty of the fjords and mountains, while also revealing the startling vastness. We should issue a small piece of advice for CURVES Norway here: don't make the mistake of assuming that the spectacular scenes of the trip are easy to experience or that they are concentrated in a specific area. The long straight roads and hard-won miles between sensations are also part of what makes Norway. This is a country for advanced travellers. Wanderlust and a search for pure driving pleasure atuned to the beat of the CURVES rhythm, will be satisfied here. By the way, as drivers who measure things in terms of sports car categories, we realize one thing: here in Norway the car, that magical machine of freedom, is the only way to reach the most beautiful spots. Norway is so huge that almost nothing is possible without a car. Cyclists would need impossibly long legs get anywhere, and motorcyclists would have to have buns of steel. However you decide to undertake the journey, experience Norway with us now. *Soulful driving.*

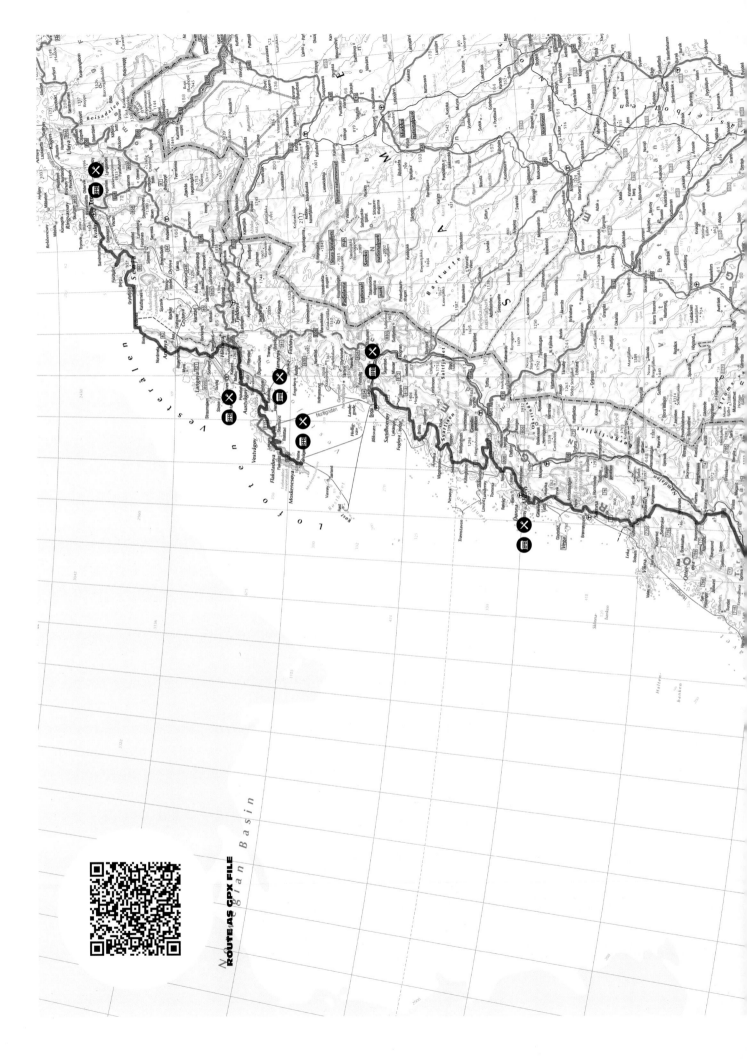

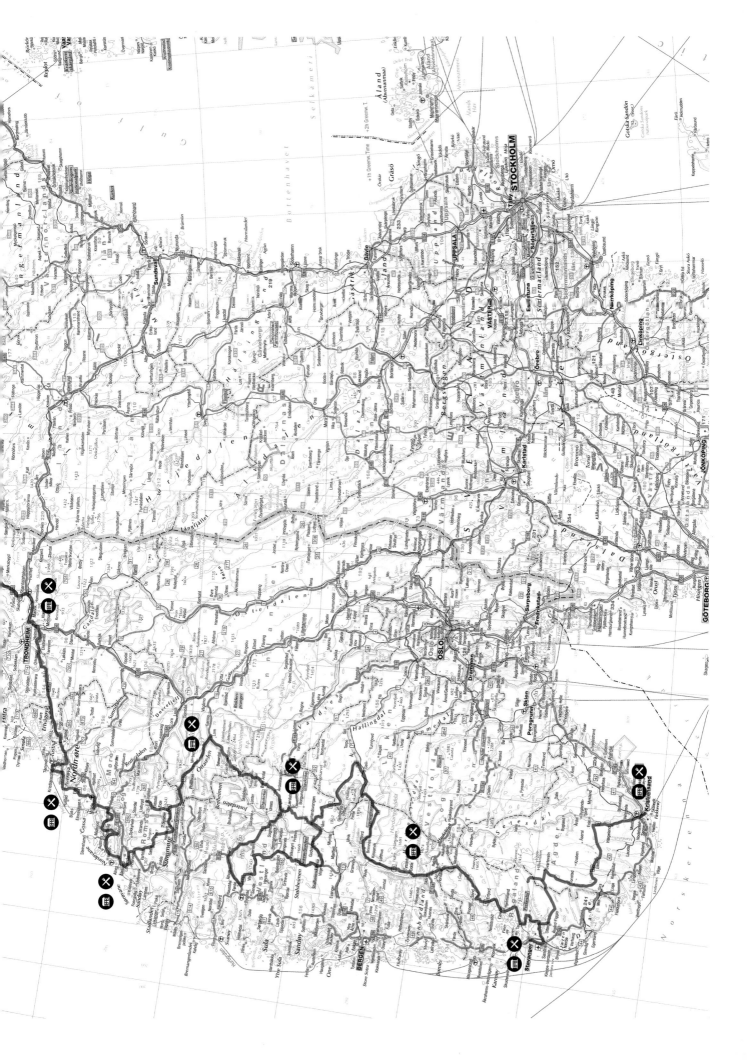

HYTEHAUGEN

ETAPPE STAGE

ETAPPE STAGE

Weit im Norden beginnt die Reise: Zwischen Nordkap und Lofoten versteckt sich Tromsø tief in einem Fjord der norwegischen Küste, hier hat man es nicht weit nach Schweden oder Finnland – bis zur norwegischen Hauptstadt Oslo sind es hingegen über 1.600 Kilometer. Das Land rund um Tromsø bietet mit seinen Inseln, Bergen und Meeresarmen einen ersten Vorgeschmack auf den Charakter der kommenden Reise-Etappen. Wir wollen hinüber zu den vorgelagerten Lofoten-Inseln und könnten dafür eine ruhigere Inlandsroute wählen, setzen aber auf die ausgesetztere Variante entlang der Küste. Um hier voranzukommen, müssen alle Register gezogen werden: Brücken und Tunnel führen von Insel zu Insel, langwierige Fjord-Umrundungen werden durch spektakuläre Ausblicke belohnt, immer wieder führen nur noch Fährlinien weiter. Vom Gryllefjord bis zur Insel Andøya ist eine der ersten langen Fährverbindungen zu erwarten und im Süden der Lofoten angekommen wissen wir, dass sich der weite Weg gelohnt hat: Mit andächtig machender Schönheit endet die erste Etappe bei Reine und am Hafen von Moskenes.

Our journey begins far in the north: Tromsø is hidden deep in a fjord on the Norwegian coast between the North Cape and Lofoten. It is not far from here to Sweden or Finland, but, on the other hand, it is over 1,600 kilometers to the Norwegian capital, Oslo. The country around Tromsø, with its islands, mountains and inlets, offers a first taste of the upcoming stages of the journey. Our plan is to cross over to the offshore Lofoten Islands and we could choose a quieter inland route to do this, but decide on the more exposed coastal route. In order to make progress here, we need to pull out all the stops: bridges and tunnels lead from island to island; long circuits of fjords are rewarded with spectacular views; time and again ferry services are the only way to continue our trip. We expected one of the first long ferry connections would be from the Gryllefjord to the island of Andøya, and when we arrive in southern Lofoten we know that the long journey was worth it: the first stage ends at Reine and the awe-inspiring beauty of the port of Moskenes.

Mit der Mammut-Etappe von Bødo bis Ålesund schlagen wir einen über 1.000 Kilometer weiten Bogen vom Tor zu den Lofoten bis in den Südwesten Norwegens. Von jenseits des Polarkreises bis zu den majestätischen Fjorden. Und zugegeben: Es gibt Momente auf dieser Fahrt, in denen man sich wünscht, schon angekommen zu sein, einfach weil der Weg so weit ist. Und Norwegen macht es einem nicht leicht: Im Labyrinth der Inseln und Meeresarme zählt jeder Kilometer doppelt. Und trotzdem bereuen wir die hier verbrachten Stunden nicht: Die leuchtende Schönheit der norwegischen Atlantik-Küste wird niemals zur Wiederholung, der Spannungsbogen bricht nicht. Handfeste Gründe auf diese „Reise in der Reise" zu gehen, gibt es durchaus: Nur so lassen sich die Lofoten auf Achse erleben. Wer dort oben sein und nicht fliegen möchte, muss fahren. Und die Mahlströme rund um den Saltfjorden sind für sich allein eine Reise wert. Das unaufhörliche Fähren-und-Insel-Hopping entlang der Küstenlinie ebenfalls. Es entsteht ein eigentümlicher Groove aus Fahren und Warten, der einen geduldig und demütig macht, das muss man erlebt haben. Und wenn man dann nach Kristiansund am Atlanterhavsveien ankommt, ist das wie eine Verheißung auf kommende Abenteuer, die den zurückliegenden Kilometern Sinn geben und den kommenden Glanz. Wir würden es immer wieder tun.

The mammoth stage from Bødo to Ålesund covers a 1,000-kilometer arc from the gateway to the Lofoten Islands to the south-west of Norway. We travel from beyond the Arctic Circle to the majestic fjords. Admittedly there are moments on this trip when you wish were already at your destination, simply because it is such a long way. Also, Norway doesn't make things easy: in the labyrinth of islands and inlets, every kilometer counts twice. And yet we don't regret the hours we spent here: the radiant beauty of the Norwegian Atlantic coast is never to be repeated, the suspense never breaks. There are plenty of good reasons to go on this "journey within a journey": this is the only way to experience Lofoten Islands on the move. If you want get there without flying, you have to drive. The maelstroms around the Saltfjorden are enough on their own to take the trip worthwhile. The same goes for the endless ferries and island hopping along the coastline. You get into a peculiar groove of driving and waiting, which makes you patient and humble – something you have to experience to understand. And then when you arrive at Atlanterhavsveien after Kristiansund, it's like a promise of adventures to come, making sense of the distance covered and the brilliance to come. We would do it all again and again.

ETAPPE
STAGE

ETAPPE
STAGE

Aus Ålesund kommt man nur in Richtung Süden weiter, wenn man die Fähre nimmt, und das wird für die ersten Kilometer dieser Etappe ein prägendes Element bleiben: Unterwegs im Hjørundfjord, einem Seitenarm des weltberühmten Geirangerfjords, führt die Straße nur ungefähr bis zur Hälfte, ab dann geht es nur auf dem Schiff weiter. Der Geirangerfjord schiebt sich derweil nördlich durch die Berge, bei Hellesylt haben wir ihn nach einer Überquerung des dazwischenliegenden Bergkamms erreicht, und auch er macht ein Vorankommen auf der Straße unmöglich: Nur per Fähre kann man Geiranger von Westen her erreichen. Über die sogenannte Adlerstraße verlassen wir den Fjord nach Norden, wechseln zum Tafjord und fahren dann über den Valldal-Nationalpark zum Trollstigen. Die spektakuläre Serpentinenstraße ist hier das Tor zum Romsdalsfjord bei Åndalsnes. Unsere Route führt aber zurück nach Geiranger, und von dort über den Dalsnibba-Pass nach Südosten, hinaus aus der Provinz Møre og Romsdal, über einen Abschnitt durch Innlandet in die Provinz Vestland. Am Lærdalsfjord haben wir das Ziel der Etappe beinahe erreicht, schließen aber noch zwei Entdeckungsreisen zum Stegastein-Aussichtspunkt und ins nahe gelegene Borgund-Tal an.

The only way south from Ålesund is to take the ferry. This will remain a defining element for the first few kilometers of this stage: as we travel along the Hjørundfjord, a side arm of the world-famous Geirangerfjord, the road only takes you half way before you have to transfer to ship. The Geirangerfjord meanwhile pushes north through the mountains. We reach it at Hellesylt, having crossed the intervening ridge, and find it impossible to go any further by road: Geiranger can only be reached from the west by ferry. We leave the fjord to the north via the so-called Eagle Road, switching to the Tafjord and then driving via the Valldal National Park to the Trollstigen. The spectacular serpentine road here is the gateway to the Romsdalsfjord at Åndalsnes. However, our route takes us back to Geiranger, and from there over the Dalsnibba pass south-east, out of Møre og Romsdal province, via a section through Innlandet into Vestland province. Arriving at the Lærdalsfjord we have almost reached the final destination of this stage, although two journeys of discovery still await us: the Stegastein lookout point and the nearby Borgund Valley.

Rund um die zwei großen Fjorde des norwegischen Westens bewegen wir uns auf der vierten Etappe – die Reise beginnt am Sognefjord. Auf einem weiten Bogen nach Norden dringen wir bis zu den Ausläufern des Jostedalsbreen vor: Die mächtige Gletscherhaube bedeckt nach wie vor große Gebiete im Landesinneren, allerdings trägt auch hier der Klimawandel stark zu einem deutlichen Abschmelzen des Eises bei. Entlang des großen Jølstravatnet-Sees rollen wir nun nach Westen, vollenden dann unsere Runde zurück zum Sognefjord. Über den Vikafjelsvegen und dann die E 16 nach Osten landen wir bei Flåm und damit beinahe wieder am Ausgangspunkt. Von hier aus ziehen wir aber an Steine vorüber weiter ins Landesinnere zurück, fahren in die Region Viken und schlagen erst bei Hagafoss erneut einen Haken. Nun geht es über die Seeenlandschaft südlich des Haugastøl, die nördlichen Ausläufer der Hardangervidda-Hochebene und die tiefen Taleinschnitte in der Region rund um den Vøringfossen zum zweiten Fjord-Riesen der norwegischen Westküste: dem Hardangerfjord. Entlang seines Sørfjord-Ausläufers zielen wir nun geradewegs nach Süden, bis wir in der von Halbinseln und Inseln geprägten Küstenlandschaft rund um Stavanger angekommen sind. Hier, in der viertgrößten Stadt Norwegens, haben wir den Ausgangspunkt zur letzten Etappe erreicht.

On the fourth stage of our trip, we circumnavigate the two large fjords of western Norway – the journey begins at the Sognefjord. Moving in a wide northerly arc, we advance to the foothills of the Jostedalsbreen glacier: the mighty glacial cap still covers large inland areas, but climate change is also making a significant contribution to significant melting of the ice here. We now travel west along the expanse of Jølstravatnet Lake, completing our trip by looping back to the Sognefjord. Following the Vikafjelsvegen route and then the E 16 to the east we end up at Flåm and thus almost back at our starting point. From here, however, we turn back further inland across stones, traveling into the Viken region only to make another detour at Hagafoss. We now cross the lake-filled landscape south of the Haugastøl, the northern foothills of the Hardangervidda plateau and the deep valleys in the region around the Vøringfossen to reach the second gigantic fjord of the Norwegian west coast: the Hardangerfjord. We now head straight south along Sørfjord, the main fjord's little sister, until we arrive in the coastal landscape around Stavanger, characterized by numerous peninsulas and islands. Here, in Norway's fourth largest city, we have reached the starting point for the last stage of our trip.

5

**ETAPPE
STAGE**

Ungefähr auf Höhe von Stavanger endet die von Fjorden zerklüftete Westküste Norwegens. Die Stadt liegt am nördlichsten Punkt eines weiten Bogens, den die Küste von hier aus nach Osten schlägt und dann bei Kristiansand in Richtung Oslo verläuft. Unsere letzte Etappe führt über diese Südspitze Norwegens, mit einem letzten, kurvenreichen Abstecher zum Ende des Lysefjords sagen wir der Welt dieser atemberaubend schönen Meeresarme auf Wiedersehen. Übrigens: Am westlichen Ende des Lysefjord, wenige Kilometer nach seinem Beginn im Høgsfjord, liegt einer der spektakulärsten Orte Norwegens: Der 600 Meter tief zum Fjord hin frei abfallende Preikestolen (Predigtstuhl) war schon in einigen Hollywood-Filmen landschaftlicher Hauptdarsteller. Er ist nur zu Fuß zu erreichen, je nach Jahreszeit ist man zum Leidwesen von Landschaftsschützern hier auch nicht ganz allein unterwegs. Wer also den Preikestolen besuchen möchte, sollte das möglichst nicht im Sommer tun, sondern rücksichtsvoll und an einem ruhigeren Tag des Jahres. Die weitere Route zum langgezogenen Sirdalsvatnet-See, dann quer über die Berge zum Lygne-See und schließlich nach Süden, an die Küste bei Kristiansand, verläuft dagegen deutlich ruhiger. Ein letztes Mal sind wir im wilden Inland Norwegens unterwegs, dann haben wir das Ziel am Skagerrak erreicht.

Norway's west coast, which is studded with fjords, ends roughly at the level of Stavanger. The city lies at the northernmost point of a wide arc as the coast sweeps east from here and then towards Oslo at Kristiansand. The last leg of our trip takes us across this southern tip of Norway, with a final, winding detour to the end of the Lysefjord, where we say goodbye to the world of breathtakingly beautiful inlets. By the way: the western end of the Lysefjord, a few kilometers after its beginning in the Høgsfjord, is one of the most spectacular places in Norway: the 600-meter-deep Preikestolen (pulpit), which drops straight down to the fjord, has provided the backdrop for a number of Hollywood movies. It can only be reached on foot. Depending on the season, it can get quite busy here, much to the chagrin of the conservationists. So, if you want to visit the Preikestolen, you should try to avoid doing so in summer, choosing instead a quieter time of year. The route continues to the elongated expanse of Sirdalsvatnet Lake, then crosses the mountains to Lake Lygne and finally heads south to the coast at Kristiansand and is much quieter. One last time we take a route that passes through the wild interior of Norway, before reaching our destination at the Skagerrak.

LYSEBOTN

EDITORIAL

Wer Europa kennenlernen will, und vielleicht sogar etwas über das Werden des sogenannten Westens, der fängt im Norden an. Hoch oben unter den flirrenden Polarlichtern des Winters und an schier endlosen Sommertagen. Zwischen atlantischer Felsenküste, mächtigen Fjorden und schroffen Inlands-Gebirgen. In Norwegen.

Man sagt, das Land trage seinen Namen, weil es eben am Ende aller Wege liegt, die nach Norden führen, eine andere Deutung gefällt uns aber besser: In altem Skandinavisch ist ein „Nor" ein enger Fjord – und aus der CURVES-Perspektive betrachtet ist nichts „norwegischer" als das stetige Fahren von Wasser zu Wasser. Von Brücke zu Brücke. Von Fähre zu Fähre. – Die Küste Norwegens zerbröselt zu unzähligen Inseln, wird von tief einschneidenden Buchten und viele Kilometer weit reichenden Fjorden aufgebrochen. Die von Eiszeit-Gletschern zerriebenen, bewaldeten Hügellandschaften und riesenhaften Berge des Landes drängen sich bis an diese volatile Küstenlinie heran, lassen zwischen sich und dem Meer nur wenig Raum, in dem sich Menschen ausbreiten könnten. Und genau deshalb zieht die Straße aus dem äußersten Norden immer entlang des Meeres. Springt dabei über unzählige Brücken, große und kleine. Schlängelt sich entlang der zerklüfteten Küstenlinie, führt hinauf und hinab, erkämpft sich jeden Meter nach Süden in unermüdlichem Slalom. Und wenn sie sich dann in diesem Irrgarten aus Felsen im Meer wieder einmal bis ans Ende einer Inselgruppe verfahren hat, wie sie es eigentlich dauernd tut, schlägt ganz bestimmt eine Fähre die Verbindung ans nächste Ufer. Und weiter geht es. Übers Wasser. Am Wasser. Von Stein zu Stein hüpfend. Wege über die „Nor". Unterwegs auf diesen „Nor-Wegen", durch ein wunderschönes, aber überbordend wildes und kaum zu bändigendes Land, versteht man dann auch, weshalb von hier ein wahrer Schockimpuls für ganz Europa ausgegangen ist, den wir alle kennen, aber heute nur selten richtig einordnen. Ganz ohne Übertreibung: Norwegen ist in Europa beinahe überall. Von hier hat sich ein trockener Menschenschlag auf den Weg in die Welt gemacht und sie von Grund auf verändert: die Wikinger. Sie waren Dänen und Schweden, vor allem aber Norweger, die von den kargen Küsten Skandinaviens in See stachen und Europa prägten. Vielleicht muss diese alte Geschichte erzählt werden, um unserer Reise durch Norwegen einen verborgenen roten Faden zu geben. Weil selbst der CURVES-Reiselust, die uns hierherge-

If you want to get to know Europe, and maybe even something about the development of the so-called western world, the north is a good place to start, in a place of shimmering Northern Lights in winter and seemingly endless summer days. Between the rocky Atlantic coast, mighty fjords and rugged inland mountains. In Norway.

The story goes that the country got its name because it lies at the end of all roads north, but we like another interpretation better: in old Scandinavian, a "Nor" is a narrow fjord, and, from the CURVES perspective, there is nothing more "Norwegian" than constantly driving from water to water, bridge to bridge and ferry to ferry. The coast of Norway disintegrates into countless islands, broken up by deeply fissured bays and fjords that stretch for many kilometers. Crushed by Ice Age glaciers, the country's forested hillsides and towering mountains push up against this volatile coastline, leaving little room between them and the sea for people to spread themselves. That's exactly why the road from the extreme north always follows the sea, jumping over countless bridges, large and small. It meanders along the rugged coastline, climbing up and down, battling every meter of the way south in a relentless slalom. And when the road has once again made its way through this maze of rocks in the sea to the end of a group of islands, as it does all the time, you can be sure that a ferry will be available to take you to the opposite shore. And so we journey on. On the water. By the water. Hopping from stone to stone. Finding our way "Nor". As you travel along the highways and byways of Norway's beautiful, but wild and almost untamable countryside, you begin to understand why this was the birthplace of a real shock for the whole of Europe that we all know about, but that we rarely classify correctly today. It is no exaggeration to say that there is something of Norway to be found almost throughout Europe. From here, a dry-witted breed of people made their way into the world, changing it from the ground up: the Vikings. They were Danes and Swedes, but mostly Norwegians, who set sail from the barren shores of Scandinavia and shaped the evolution of Europe. Perhaps this ancient story needs to be told to provide a secret thread to our journey through Norway. After all, even the CURVES wanderlust that brought us here has a tiny spark of the same adventurous northern spirit. As well as colorful volumes about dinosaurs, knights and pirates, every child's room always has a book about Vikings. Norsemen have become synonymous with adventure. But

bracht hat, ein kleiner Funke innewohnt, der von hier oben stammt. In jedem Kinderzimmer steht gleich neben bunten Büchern über Dinosaurier, Ritter und Piraten auch eines über die Wikinger. Die Nordmänner sind zu einem Synonym für Abenteuerlust geworden. Wer sie aber auf ihren Mythos reduziert, versteht kaum, wie immens der Beitrag der Wikinger wirklich war – und immer noch ist. Dass sie zwischen 793 und ungefähr 880 n. Chr. in vielen Zügen große Landstriche des heutigen Englands eroberten und dann zunehmend ein Teil der heutigen angelsächsischen Kultur wurden, wissen viele. Dass die Wikinger Island besiedelten, sich auf Grönland niederließen und bis nach Nordamerika fuhren, ist ebenfalls ein mit Bewunderung weitergeraunter Fakt.

Dass die mehrfach Paris belagernden Nordmänner später der heutigen Normandie ihren Namen gaben und Untertanen des französischen Königs wurden, könnte ebenfalls die eine oder der andere ahnen. Aber dass es die Wikinger über die Ostsee und die Flüsse des Ostens bis ins Schwarze und Kaspische Meer schafften, als „Waräger" gar die Leibwache des byzantinischen Kaisers stellten, wissen nur wenige. Und wer hat schon einmal davon gehört, dass Wikinger in den Städten am Niederrhein und an der Mosel Schrecken verbreiteten? Dass sie Hamburg, Köln, Trier, Lissabon, Cádiz, Sevilla, Nowgorod und sogar Baku brandschatzten? Oder nach einer mehrere Generationen dauernden Kampagne im heutigen Italien sesshaft wurden? Von Raub-Horden und gekauften Söldnern zu Herzögen und Fürsten mit päpstlichem Segen aufstiegen, ganze Provinzen der italienischen Halbinsel bevölkerten und regierten, gar den Sarazenen Sizilien streitig machten? – Überall gekommen, um zu bleiben. Das Bild von lediglich rauflustigen Abenteuer-Horden ist also nicht nur äußerst einseitig, sondern in seiner Vereinfachung schlichtweg falsch. Wer heute die Wikinger als Archetypen vorchristlicher, naturnaher Gesellschaften ansieht und damit romantisierend-reaktionären Vorstellungen einen bärtigen Helden verpassen möchte, liegt völlig daneben: Die Wikinger haben Europa modernisiert. Vermutlich haben wir ihnen unsere Offenheit und Reiselust zu verdanken, unsere Toleranz und positiven Opportunismus und, wer weiß, vermutlich auch unseren Individualismus. Die Nordmänner (und -frauen!) waren bemerkenswert modern, viel weniger patriarchal, als sie es zu ihrer Zeit hätten sein dürfen, ihre Gesellschaften beinahe demokratisch organisiert, an flachen Hierarchien und flexiblen Strukturen

if you reduce them to this level of myth, you risk overlooking how immense the contribution of the Vikings really was – and still is. Many people know that between 793 and about 880 AD they conquered large swathes of what is now England in numerous campaigns and then increasingly became a part of today's Anglo-Saxon culture. The fact that the Vikings settled Iceland and Greenland and traveled as far as North America is also a source of great admiration. People might also guess that the men of the north who besieged Paris several times later gave their name to today's Normandy and became subjects of the French king. But few are aware that the Vikings made it across the Baltic Sea and the rivers of the East to the Black Sea and Caspian Sea, when the "Varaigians" even provided the bodyguard of the Byzantine Emperor. And who has ever heard of Vikings spreading terror in the towns on the Lower Rhine and Moselle? Who knew that they burned Hamburg, Cologne, Trier, Lisbon, Cadiz, Seville, Novgorod and even Baku? Or that they settled in present-day Italy after a campaign lasting several generations, rising from robber bands and hired mercenaries to dukes and princes with papal blessings, populating and governing entire provinces of the Italian peninsula, even competing for Sicily with the Saracens? – Whenever they arrived, they came to stay.

The image of hordes of scrap-happy adventurers is not only extremely one-sided, but simply wrong in its over-simplification. Anyone who regards the Vikings as archetypes of pre-Christian, nature-led societies and who seeks a bearded hero for their romanticizing-reactionary ideas will seek in vain: the Vikings modernized Europe. We probably have them to thank for our openness and desire to travel, our tolerance and positive opportunism and, who knows, probably also our sense of individualism. The men and women of the north were remarkably modern, much less patriarchal than you'd expect for their day, their societies organized almost democratically, built around flat hierarchies and flexible structures. This was one of their most tempting and turbulent imports wherever they chose to settle. You could say they lit a fuse under the idea of staying at home and sticking to what you know. Hence, if you look closely, you can still somehow see traces of Nordic ways in Europe. It is quite amazing to think that all of these upheavals in the human world were set in motion by a wild and barren country that simply could not offer enough space or a decent livelihood for many of its population.

entlang aufgebaut. Und das haben sie als turbulente Versuchung eingebracht, wo immer sie sesshaft wurden. Sozusagen eine Lunte gelegt, ans Stubenhocken und ans Altbackene. Wer also genau hinsieht, erkennt in Europa immer noch Spuren des Nordens. Nord-Wege, irgendwie eben doch. Dass all diese Umwälzungen der Menschenwelt aber durch ein wildes und karges Land in Gang gesetzt wurden, das einfach nicht genug Raum und Auskommen für Viele bot, ist das eigentlich Verblüffende. Eigentlich mehr als offensichtlich und dabei doch eine Erzählung, die sich gut versteckt: Wer heute in Norwegen den langen Weg vom Nordkap nach Süden antritt, wird selbstverständlich keine Geschichtsstunde erleben. Aber sehen, wie kilometerhohe Eiszeitgletscher die Erdkruste darunter geschliffen und zerfurcht haben, blanken Fels übrig ließen. Kein fettes Land. Wie dann das Meer mit diesem Land ringt: Heben und Senken, als jahrmillionenlangsamer Erdkrusten-Engtanz. Wie sich nun keine fruchtbaren Ebenen und leicht zugänglichen Wege auftun, sondern fürchterliche Felswände in tiefschwarze Fjorde fallen und sich auch noch unter den Wasseroberflächen in gähnenden Abgründen fortsetzen. Wie lange Winter und kurze Sommer eine Vegetation einhegen, die eher trotzig als üppig ist und knorrig als fruchtbar. Bei aller Schönheit ist eines klar: Hier im Norden gewinnt man nicht, man passt sich klug an.

Diese Erkenntnis macht Norwegen aus. Demut und Erfindungsreichtum gehen hier Hand in Hand. Man packt an, definiert sich aber nicht über Leistung und Erfolg, sondern über das Sein. Man kultiviert einen lässigen Optimismus, setzt aber gleichzeitig äußerst hartnäckig auf konsequente Chancenverwertung. „Out-of-the-box"-Denken spricht Norwegisch – ganz bei sich bleiben aber auch. Dass sich die Norweger bis zum Chef des Chefs hinauf duzen, darf auch heute noch als Nachbeben alter Wikinger-Weisen gelten: Es handelt sich hier nicht um Respektlosigkeit oder belangloses Ankumpeln, sondern um eine eigentlich selbstverständliche Größenangleichung der Hierarchien, bei gleichzeitiger Beibehaltung eines gesunden Abstands zum Gegenüber. Sowieso darf man nicht dem Irrtum verfallen, der ausgeprägte Individualismus der Norweger und ihre Liebe zu flachen Hierarchien seien als Beziehungslosigkeit oder Ausdruck

Even though the facts are more than obvious, this is a well-hidden story: of course anyone who starts the long journey from the North Cape to the south in Norway today should not expect a history lesson. But seeing the way Ice Age glaciers miles high have eroded and furrowed the earth's crust beneath, leaving bare rock behind tells you this is not a place where you could live off the fat of the land. The same goes for the way the sea wrestles with the land, rising and sinking, performing a slow, close dance with the earth's crust over a period of millions of years. Likewise you notice the lack of fertile plains and easily accessible transport routes, seeing instead fearsome rock walls that drop into deep black fjords, continuing under the water's surface as yawning abysses. It is evident how long winters and short summers impact on vegetation, making it more defiant than lush, more gnarled than fertile. Despite all the beauty on show, one thing is clear: here in the north you don't win against the elements, you just adapt judiciously.

This realization is what makes Norway what it is. Humility and inventiveness go hand in hand here. You get things done, but you don't define yourself by performance or success, but rather by being. You cultivate a casual optimism, but at the same time you tenaciously rely on the consistent exploitation of opportunities. "Out-of-the-box" thinking is quintessentially Norwegian, but so is maintaining a sense of proportion. The fact that the Norwegians habitually use informal speech patterns at all hierarchical levels can still be seen as an echo of old Viking wisdom: there is no element of disrespect or inappropriate over-familiarity here, but instead an expression of the self-evident equality of hierarchies, while at the same time maintaining a healthy distance toward the other person. In any case, one should not fall into the trap of misinterpreting the distinct individualism of the Norwegians and their love for flat hierarchies as a lack of warmth or a sign of poor community spirit. A clue can be found in the Norwegians' dress code: in Norway, people usually dress casually and functionally for everyday life – however as soon as there are festivities or community events to attend, people bring out their bow ties, suits and evening dresses. This is not for themselves, but for others. Simply because others are important. Norwegians rarely confuse

„Draußen" ist das eigentliche Wohnzimmer der Norweger, man fischt, angelt, wandert, segelt oder fährt Ski. Wetter in allen Aggregatzuständen wird höchstens als Kulisse betrachtet, kaum als Hindernis.

The "Great Outdoors" is where most Norwegians live their lives, fishing, angling, hiking, sailing or skiing. The weather in its many forms is viewed mostly as a backdrop and rarely as an obstacle.

mangelnden Gemeinsinns zu interpretieren. Ein Fingerzeig findet sich in norwegischen Kleiderordnungen: Den Alltag bestreitet man in Norwegen meist leger und funktional bekleidet – sobald aber Festivitäten oder Gemeinschafts-Veranstaltungen zu absolvieren sind, trägt man Fliege, Krawatte, Anzug, Abendkleid und Co. Nicht für sich – für die anderen. Weil die wichtig sind. Individualismus verwechseln Norweger selten mit Egoismus. Auch deshalb sollte man sich in Norwegen (und ja, nicht nur da ...) Wichtigtuerei abgewöhnen. Skandinavische Gesellschaften kennen keine Stars und keine Angeber.

Weil aber in Norwegen die Natur bei allem menschlichen Sein und Tun stets ein gewichtiges Wörtchen mitredet, bisweilen sogar das letzte Wort oder wenigstens ein Veto-Recht hat, sind die Norweger zu einer Natur-Beziehung gewechselt, die größtenteils respektvoll und auf Augenhöhe ist. „Draußen" ist das eigentliche Wohnzimmer der Norweger, man fischt, angelt, wandert, segelt oder fährt Ski. Wetter in allen Aggregatzuständen wird höchstens als Kulisse betrachtet, kaum als Hindernis. Und weil in Norwegen das sogenannte „Jedermannsrecht" gilt, nach dem man sich überall frei bewegen und aufhalten darf, gibt es nicht einmal private Strände oder von öffentlichem Zugang abgeschottete Seeufer.

Natürlich dürfte dem Reisenden aber eine andere, ganz irdische Angelegenheit mindestens ebenso am Herzen liegen wie die „Jedermannsrecht"-Freizügigkeit, und zwar eine kulinarische Landkarte Norwegens. Die ist der geografischen Karte ausgesprochen ähnlich, verbindet Fisch und Fleisch, Gemüse und Obst aus saisonaler Einfachheit, robustes Getreide sowie habhafte Soßen und schätzt – wer hätte es gedacht – Gerichte aus Haltbargemachtem: Käse, Dörrfisch und -fleisch, Brot. Nur das Spektakuläre der norwegischen Fjorde geht der Küche des skandinavischen Westens ab, im Regelfall wird mit überschaubarer Finesse gekocht. Es geht ums Sattwerden, um Soulfood im allerbesten Sinn, und wer diese Elemente mag, dürfte in Norwegen auch kulinarisch ankommen. Zwischen Bergen, Fjorden und dem Meer. In einem Land von bemerkenswerter Schönheit, aber ohne jeden Show-Effekt. Echt. Norwegen.

individualism with egotism. That's one of the reasons why there's little tolerance of self-importance in Norway (if only it were the same elsewhere...). Scandinavian society has no time for divas or blow-hards. However, because nature always has a say in everything humans do in Norway, sometimes even having the last word or at least the right of veto, Norwegians have chosen a relationship with nature that is largely respectful and on an equal footing. The "Great Outdoors" is where most Norwegians live their lives, fishing, angling, hiking, sailing or skiing. The weather in its many forms is viewed mostly as a backdrop and rarely as an obstacle. And because Norway recognizes the "right to roam", you can go anywhere and pitch camp wherever you like – there aren't even any private beaches or lake shore areas sealed off from public access. Of course, another, very earth-bound matter should be at least as important to the traveler as the freedom of movement and "right to roam", namely a culinary map of Norway. This is extremely similar to the geographical map, combining fish and meat, vegetables and fruit according to simple seasonal principles, robust grains and accessible sauces and an appreciation of dishes made from preserved foods: cheese, bread, dried fish and meat. All that is missing from the cuisine of the Scandinavian west is the spectacle of the Norwegian fjords and cooking is usually done with a degree of modesty that belies finesse. It's about filling your belly and soul food in the best sense of the word, so anyone who appreciates these elements should find culinary satisfaction in Norway. Between mountains, fjords and sea. In a country of remarkable beauty but without any attention seeking glamour. Simply genuinely Norway.

HENNINGSVÆR

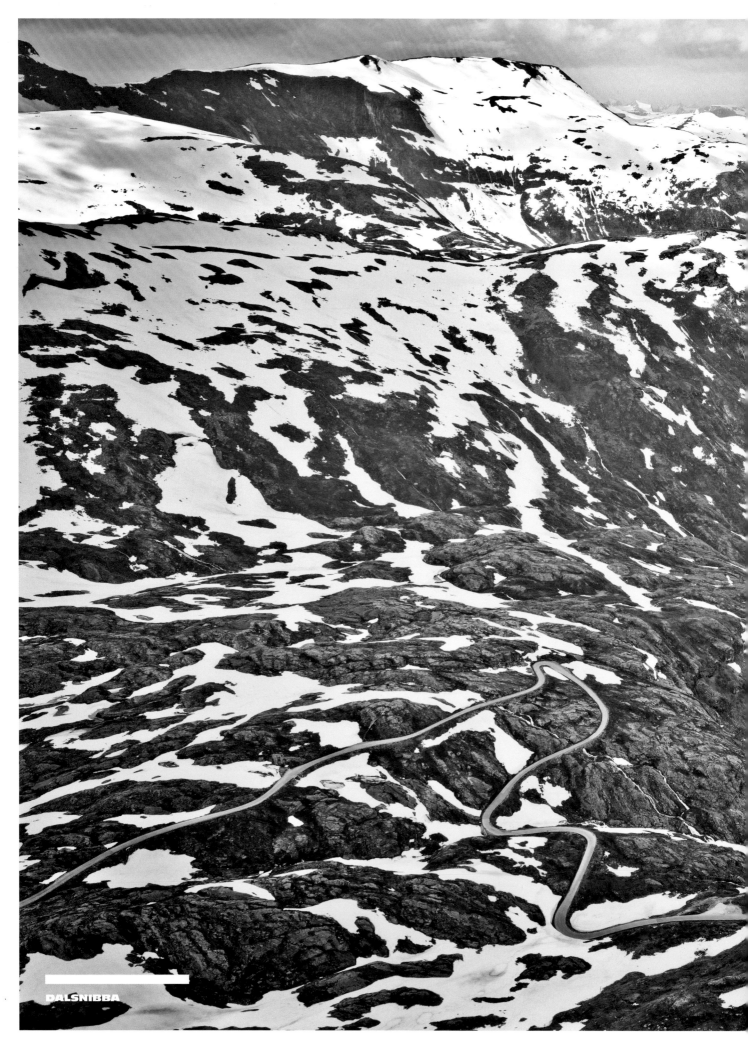

DALSNIBBA

VIDFOSSEN ROAD 13

ROAD TO HENNINGSVÆR

ROAD 63 TO GEIRANGER

RØLDALSFJELLET

ROAD 520 HARA - SAUDA

PRESTESTEINNSVATNET

ROAD 520 HARA - SAUDA

ATLANTIC ROAD

ROAD 63 · TROLLSTIGEN

LYSEBOTN

TROLLSTIGEN

ROAD E10 · TENGELFJORD

TROMSØ MOSKENES

850 KM • 3-4 TAGE // 530 MILES • 3-4 DAYS

Dreihundertfünfzig Kilometer nördlich des Polarkreises drängen sich schroffe Berge. Wie Fels-Trolle warten sie, mit von Gletschern glattgehobelten Häuptern und bis weit in den Sommer hinein bedeckt von Schneeflicken. Es scheint sie nicht zu stören, dass der Nordatlantik zwischen ihnen eingesickert ist und ihre Gipfelplateaus zu Inseln macht, zwischen denen eiskaltes Salzwasser schwarz und tief steht.

—

The craggy mountains glower at three hundred and fifty kilometers north of the Arctic Circle. They lie in wait like stony-hearted trolls, their heads smoothed by glaciers and covered in patches of snow late into the summer. It doesn't seem to bother them that the North Atlantic has seeped in between their toes, turning the plateaus on their summits into islands separated by ice-cold, deep, black salt water.

SOMMARØY

Die Berge sind hoch, aber ihr Sockel liegt tief auf dem Grund des Meeres und deshalb sind auch die Meeresarme so besonders, die die Berge umschlingen – Fjorde nennt man sie. Ein Menschenwort, das insgeheim von einer Perspektive ausgeht, in der das Land die Hauptrolle spielt und das Meer die des Eindringlings. Dabei darf das an der Küstenlinie Norwegens ganz bestimmt nicht als ausgemacht gelten: Hier kämpft die See in jahrtausendealtem Patt mit dem Gebirge, man muss bis weit ins Landesinnere fahren, um eine Welt zu finden, in der die Fjorde endlich ihren Griff lockern und ausklingen. Aus der Vogelperspektive sind die realen Verhältnisse gut zu sehen: grantige Felskuppen in einem Labyrinth aus glitzernden Meeresarmen – und wenn man sich das Wasser der Fjorde einen Moment lang wegdenkt, lägen die die Gehöfte und Dörfer und kleinen Städte der Menschen am Rand von tief hinabstürzenden Berghängen oder hoch oben in den einsamen Tälern eines mächtigen Gebirges.

Tromsø ist so eine Stadt. Gut versteckt im Landesinneren drängt sie sich auf einer Felskuppe, umgeben von Meeresarmen: Berggipfel wird zu Insel. Nach Westen führt eine Brücke, nach Osten taucht die Straße 862 unter den Fjord und landet am anderen Ufer auf dem Inselnachbarn Kvaløya, der als viele hundert Quadratkilometer großes Bergmassiv das Landesinnere rund um Tromsø vor dem Atlantik schützt. Tromsø hat auf seiner Insel Tromsøya sozusagen seinen „Sweet Spot" gefunden: beruhigender Sicherheitsabstand zum Toben des Atlantiks, verborgen in einem Irrgarten aus Wasser, aber doch mit sicherem Zugang zum offenen Meer.

Genau hier fahren wir los, unter dem blassblauen Himmel des Nordens, über den Wolken ziehen wie gigantische Schafherden. Getrieben vom Polarwind, genährt von der Sonne und dem Meer, segeln sie stetig dahin. Heute scheint ein guter Tag für Wolkenherden zu sein, die weißen Riesen wogen unablässig, wechseln dabei unaufhörlich Gestalt und Farbe. Klotzen in strahlendem Weiß, türmen sich in bedrohlichem Stahlgrau, zerfasern dann zu lichten Schleiern. Beinahe sieht es so aus, als ob sie an den Berggipfeln des Inselplateaus im Westen hängenbleiben würden, dort oben

The mountains are high, but their bases lie way down on the sea bed, which is what makes the sea inlets, or fjords, that surround these mountains so special. Fjord, a simple monosyllable that starts from an assumption that the land plays the leading role, while the ocean acts as marauding invader. The situation is certainly fluid on the coast of Norway, where the sea fights a millennia-old battle with the mountains, wrestling them to a stalemate. You have to travel far inland to find a place where the fjords finally loosen their grip and start to recede. The actual conditions are easy to spot from a bird's eye view, as aggressive rocky outcrops form a labyrinth of glittering inlets. If you stop for a moment and imagine away the water filling the fjords, the human habitats, villages and small towns would lie on the edge of vertiginous slopes, or high up in the lonely valleys of a mighty mountain range.

Tromsø is just such a town. Hidden away in the country's interior, it is crammed onto a rocky outcrop, surrounded by sea inlets: mountain peaks become islands. A bridge leads to the west, while to the east Highway 862 dives under the fjord and emerges on the far shore on the neighboring island of Kvaløya. This is a mountain massif covering many hundred square kilometers that protects the interior of Tromsø from the Atlantic Ocean. You could say that Tromsø has found the "sweet spot" on the island of Tromsøya, at a reassuringly safe distance from the raging Atlantic, hidden in a watery maze, yet with safe access to the open sea.

This is the starting point for our journey, under the pale blue northern sky and shifting clouds like huge flocks of sheep. Driven by the polar winds, nourished by the sun and sea, they sail blithely by.

Today seems to be a good day for cloud watching, as the white giants undulate constantly, changing shape and color. Blocks of radiant white whirl into menacing columns of steel gray, before fraying at the edges to produce thin veils of mist. It almost seems as if the clouds will snag on the mountain tops of the island plateau to the west, where snow still lies even in summer. Or maybe those are in fact clouds we're seeing splayed on the hilltops, like the stranded moist

HOTELS

RADISSON BLU HOTEL
SJOGATA 7, 9259 TROMSO
WWW.RADISSONHOTELS.COM

SCANDIC ISHAVSHOTEL
FREDRIK LANGESGT. 2
9250 TROMSO
WWW.SCANDICHOTELS.NO

HUSØY

HUSØY

HUSØY

liegt auch jetzt noch im Sommer Schnee. Oder sind das doch Wolken, die auf den Kuppen lagern, als klamme, gestrandete Reste des Winters? Schnee, Wasser, Dampf – ja, denken wir, irgendwie stimmt es schon, dass die Eisreste an den Hängen einfach nur faule Nachzügler sind, die für eine Auszeit dort oben fläzen. Im Norden Norwegens ist Wasser einfach überall: die Fjorde, die Wolken, der Regen, der Schnee. Unten und oben – Wasser. Genau jetzt ist das Wasser aber links: Die 862 tastet sich am Rand des Grøtsunds entlang nach Südwesten. Dann schwingt sie sich über einen Sattel zum Kaldfjorden auf der anderen Inselseite, trippelt ein paar hundert Meter ratlos am nächsten Ufer weiter und hat nun endlich gefunden, was sie gesucht hat: Die Straße in Richtung Sommarøy, hinauf ins Gebirge. In einer Rinne zwischen Bergkämmen strebt sie dann dahin, und jetzt setzen sich nach den ersten Kilometern die Gedanken. Ordnen, sortieren, vergleichen: Ist diese Welt hier oben ein klein wenig wie Schottland? Wie Island? Wie die Hochtäler der Alpen? Es dauert nicht lang, bis auch diese Frage geklärt ist, denn der Fylkjesvei 862 verliert Höhe, segelt im Tal nach unten – und sichtet Wasser. Weit und glitzernd schiebt sich wieder das Meer heran und unsere alpinen Momente zerstäuben schlagartig. Das Land an und zwischen den Fjorden ist einzigartig und völlig anders als alles bisher Bekannte. Berge mit Meer – man kann es theoretisch verstehen, begreifen aber nur dann, wenn man nach einer Fahrt über den ersten Gebirgssattel wieder am Salzwasser gelandet ist. Eben noch hoch oben in den Bergen und nun auf null Meter über Meereshöhe. Schneegipfel unter denen Wale schwimmen.

Plötzlich meinen wir das Rätsel dieser Landschaft gefunden zu haben, träumen von einem majestätischen Roadtrip in weiten Schwüngen, mit einem gelegentlichen Blick auf die Kompassnadel. Aber etwas stimmt nicht ... Die Straße ist gefesselt an den Verlauf des Fjords, und der drängt nun in die völlig falsche Richtung. Dreht immer weiter bei. Erst als der schwarze Spiegel des Fjords in grauem Schlick endet, wir an seinem banalen Ende angelangt sind und die Straße unbekümmert einen Bogen ans andere Ufer schlägt, um dort einen Ausweg in die gewünschte Himmelsrichtung zu suchen, verfängt die zweite Lektion dieser Reise im hohen Norden: Wenn es keinen Weg übers Wasser gibt, muss man darum herumfahren. Und das dauert. Vom ersten Treffen mit dem Fjord bis an dieselbe Stelle am anderen Ufer – viele Kilometer. Kurze „Norwege" sind Umwege. Um den Fjord. Ein klein wenig fühlt sich das an wie Blinde Kuh für Fortgeschrittene: mit verbundenen Augen gedreht werden, bis der innere Kompass jegliche Orientierung verloren hat, dann den Weg durch ein Labyrinth finden und die ganze Zeit nie den Glauben ans Ankommen verlieren. Als wir beim kleinen Weiler Brensholmen ankommen und dort an einem Fährkai stranden, ist das eine Mischung aus Kapitulation und Erleichterung: Anscheinend gibt es keine Möglichkeit von hier auf dem Landweg nach Süden weiterzufahren, aber

remnants of winter? Snow, water, vapor – yes, you think, somehow it makes sense that the icy patches on the slopes are just lazy straggler clouds lounging about up there, taking a break. Northern Norway is all about water: the fjords, the clouds, the rain, the snow. Water, water, everywhere. Right now the water is to our left: Highway 862 tentatively forges a path south-west along the edge of the Grøtsundet strait. It then swings over a saddle to Kaldfjorden on the other side of the island, tripping along aimlessly for another few hundred meters along the next shore before finally finding what it was looking for: the road for Sommarøy, up into the mountains. Passing through a gully between mountain ridges, the road then pushes onward and begins to settle down after the first few kilometers. Time to compare and contrast: isn't this highland world a little like Scotland? Or Iceland? Or the high valleys of the Alps?

It doesn't take long for that question to be resolved, too, as Fylkjesvei 862 drops in height to sail down the valley – and we spy water. Vast and glistening, the sea pushes up again insistently and our alpine reverie suddenly evaporates. The land between the fjords is quite unique and unlike anything we've seen so far. Mountains and sea – you can understand it in theory, but you really only grasp it when you encounter salt water again after a ride over the first mountain saddle. Although you've just been high up in the mountains, now you're at sea level. The sight of whales swimming beneath snow-capped peaks is unforgettable. Suddenly we think we have solved the riddle of this landscape, dreaming of a majestic road trip of wide arcs that require only an occasional glance at the compass needle. But something is not quite right... The road sticks close to the outline of the fjord and now starts heading in completely the wrong direction, constantly twisting. We only come to a rather banal end when the black mirror of the fjord peters out into gray mud and the road casually curves toward the far bank in search of a way out. Finally we cotton on to a second lesson on this journey in the far north: if there's no way across the water, you have to drive around it. That takes time. You often have to drive many kilometers to reach the corresponding spot on the opposite side of the fjord. This is going to be a journey of constant detours as we circumnavigate the ragged coastline. It feels a bit like an advanced game of blind man's buff: continuously turning until your internal compass has lost all sense of direction, then plotting a course through a labyrinth and all the while never losing faith that you'll get there in the end. When we arrive at the small hamlet of Brensholmen and find ourselves stranded on a ferry quay, we feel a mixture of surrender and relief: it seems there is no way to continue south from here by land, and yet here we are. Norway evidently understands that we are reluctant to start the long way journey to Tromsø: a sizeable ferry boat rumbles towards the quay, yawns extravagantly with its bow door and regurgitates a dozen vans and pickup trucks from its belly, then starts to feel hungry again. We trundle over the

ANDENES

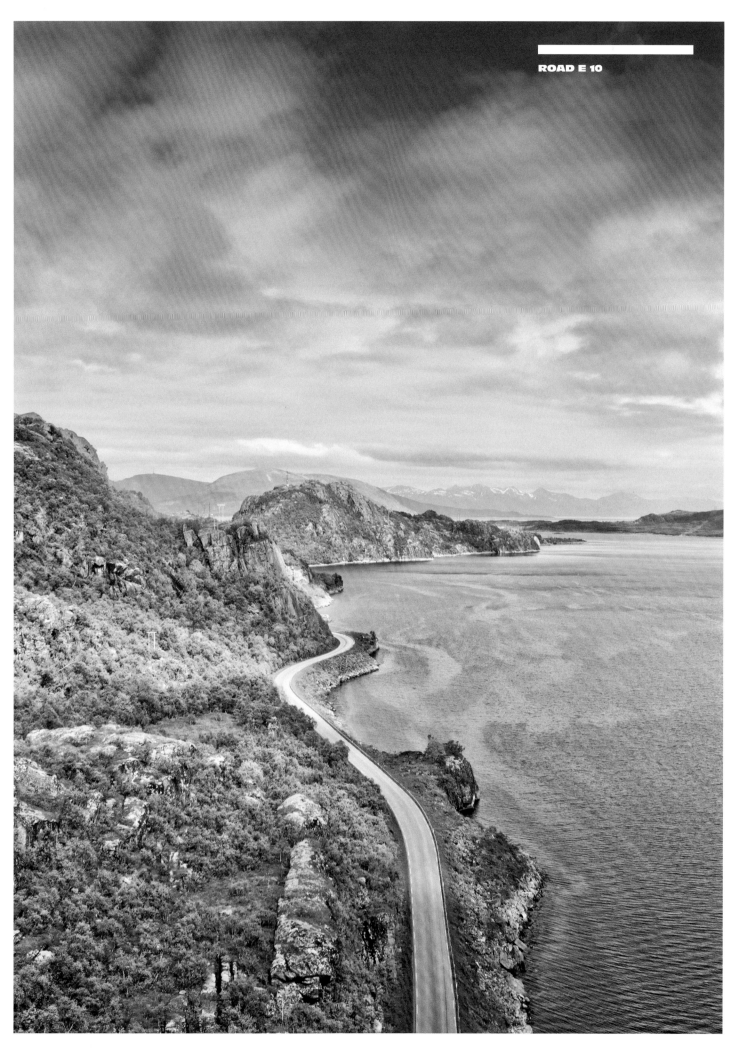

ROAD E10 · TENGELFJORD

STRAUMNES

nun sind wir hier und Norwegen hat ganz augenscheinlich Verständnis, dass wir nur ungern den mittlerweile bereits wieder langen Weg zurück nach Tromsø antreten wollen: Ein gar nicht so kleines Fährboot rumort auf den Kai zu, gähnt unanständig mit dem Bugtor, erbricht ein Dutzend Kleintransporter und Pickups, dann hat es wieder Appetit. Wir rumpeln über die Stahlrampe in den Bauch der Fähre und lassen uns zur anderen Fjord-Seite treiben. Gelassen. Entspannt. Ergeben.

Wer es hier oben eilig hat, ist auf der falschen Reise. So viel steht fest, als wir nach kurzer Fahrt in Botnhamn an Land gehen und dann weiterstromern. An den mächtigen Bergfingern der nächsten Insel entlangziehen – Fjord-ein-Fjord-aus – und am Gryllefjord schließlich wieder das Ende der Welt erreicht haben. Ende, vorbei. Auch hier geht es wieder nur per Fähre weiter und das ist an dieser Stelle tatsächlich keine so große Blamage. Schließlich sind wir nun auf der Insel Andøya angekommen, die als Teil der Vesterålen-Inselgruppe beinahe schon zu den benachbarten Lofoten gehört und damit überhaupt keine Verbindung zum Festland besitzt.

Während das wuchtige Fährboot übers Wasser des Andfjord zieht, hängen wir an der Reling und schauen wie gebannt aufs Meer hinaus: Selbst im Sommer sollen hier Pottwale an der steil abfallenden Kante des Meeresbodens nach Kraken jagen, mit etwas Glück tauchen sie ja gerade jetzt auf? – Als wir in Andenes die Fähre verlassen, haben wir aber keinen Wal gesichtet, nicht einmal der typische, schräg austretende Blas ist zu sichten. Etwas enttäuscht rollen wir durch Andenes, vorbei am kleinen Flugplatz, und biegen dann zum Raketenstartplatz Andøya ab, der sich am Fuß eines schroffen Riegels aus Bergzacken an die Küste drückt. Aber auch hier bleibt es ruhig, der Hafen zum Weltraum wirkt wie eine bessere Bushaltestelle. Ein stetiger Wind weht vom Meer heran und lässt kleine Blüten im Gras der Küstenebene tanzen. Die Welt scheint zu schlafen, in sonderbarem Standby-Modus. Wir fühlen uns gestrandet. Auf einem fremden Planeten, in einem kühlen Universum. Und mit dieser verlorenen Stimmung machen wir uns auf den Weg. Die Straße zieht im Windschat-

steel ramp into the bowels of the ferry and allow ourselves to be taken to the other side of the fjord in calm, relaxed and accepting mood. If you're in a hurry, this is definitely the wrong trip for you. That becomes clear when we go ashore in Botnhamn after a short crossing and then continue on our way. Fjord by fjord, we follow the mighty mountain fingers of the next island and finally come to a halt again at Gryllefjord, when the road runs out. Here, too, the only choice is to continue by ferry, admittedly an acceptable compromise at this point. Finally, we have reached the island of Andøya, which, as part of the Vesterålen archipelago, almost belongs to the neighboring Lofoten Islands and therefore has no connection to the mainland at all.

While the huge ferry forges its way across the water of the Andfjord, we hang over the railing and watch the sea spellbound: even in summer sperm whales are said to hunt for octopus on the steep edge of the seabed here, so, with a bit of luck, we might catch a glimpse? – By the time we disembark in Andenes, we still haven't seen any whales, not even the tell-tale oblique spray from a blowhole. Somewhat disappointed, we drive through Andenes, past the small airfield, and then turn off for the Andøya rocket launch site, which clings to the coast at the foot of a rugged bar of mountain peaks. But things seem quiet here too, the space port looking like a glorified bus terminus. A steady wind blows in from the sea, making the little flowers dance in the grass of the coastal plain. The world seems asleep, in a strange standby mode. We feel stranded on an alien planet in a cold universe. This lost mood prevails as we set off again. The road runs in the shelter of the coastal mountains. Small birches and other rugged trees stand to attention like an army of hungry soldiers on the gently rising slopes, only sometimes timidly daring to come close to the road. Our route turns southwards as a narrow strip of asphalt, then switches to the eastern side of the island and dawdles along. The fjord is blue and grey, the sky is blue and grey, far away on the horizon are the inland mountains, blue and grey.

As we cross the concrete stilts of the bridge at Risøysund to reach the island of Hinnøya, a gentle smile spreads to the corners

HOTEL & RESTAURANT

THON HOTEL LOFOTEN
TORGET, 8300 SVOLVAER
WWW.THONHOTELS.NO

HOTEL SAKRISOY GJESTEGARD
SOLBAKKEN ANNO 1880
E10 3060
8390 REINE
WWW.SAKRISOY-GJESTEGARD.COM

ANITA'S SJOMAT
SAKRISOYA
8390 REINE
WWW.SAKRISOY.NO

ROAD TO HENNINGSVÆR

TROLLFJORD

HENNINGSVÆR

ROAD TO UNSTAD

ROAD TO UNSTAD

REINE

ten des Küstengebirges dahin. Kleine Birken und andere, struppige Bäume stehen wie ein Heer von mageren Soldaten an den sanft aufstrebenden Hängen stramm, trauen sich nur manchmal ganz schüchtern bis an die Straße heran. Als schmales Asphaltband pilgert die Straße nach Süden, wechselt dann auf die Ostseite der Insel und trödelt hier immer weiter. Der Fjord ist blau und grau, der Himmel ist blau und grau, weit entfernt am Horizont ragen die Berge des Landesinneren auf, blau und grau.

Als wir an der Brücke am Risøysund auf Betonstelzen hinüber zur Insel Hinnøya streben, sickert ein sanftes Schmunzeln in unsere Mundwinkel: Wir haben die Route am Wasser gefunden. Einfach treiben lassen, die Straße sucht sich ihren Weg. Ob es die Geduldsprüfungen an den Fjord-Umrundungen sind, gemächliche Fähren, Tunnel unter Buchten und Fjorden oder Brücken – jetzt geht es voran. Links und rechts der Straße steht ein atemberaubend schönes Land Spalier: Derbe Bergmassive heben sich aus dem Meer und wandern ins Landesinnere, lichte Wälder folgen der Straße einige Kilometer weit und lassen sich dann wieder zurückfallen, dunstige Kiesstrände rücken dem Asphaltband auf die Pelle und verabschieden sich dann wieder. Je weiter wir nach Süden kommen, auf die Lofoten-Inseln, desto dramatischer wird das Schauspiel. Als ob sich die Natur alle paar Kilometer beraten hätte, wie Reisende noch sprachloser zu machen wären.

Von Svolvær traumwandeln wir über die Europastraße 10 nach Henningsvær, dem wohl einzigen Ort der Welt mit Aussichts-Fußballplatz in einer Inselsenke, hinter Leknes sind wir dann im Süden der Lofoten-Inselgruppe angelangt: Die Insel Moskenesøy ist Höhepunkt dieser ersten Etappe. Mit ihren kegelförmigen Bergen, den ins Meer gesprenkelten Inseln und tief eingeschnittenen Buchten fühlt sie sich wie das Konzentrat der zurückliegenden Kilometer an. Beim spektakulär gelegenen Reine hüpfen wir ein letztes Mal von Insel zu Insel – dann stehen wir am Hafen von Moskenes. Ende der Fahrt. Ab hier geht es für rund drei Stunden auf die Fähre ans Festland. Und dann weiter.

Links und rechts der Straße steht ein atemberaubend schönes Land Spalier: Derbe Bergmassive heben sich aus dem Meer und wandern ins Landesinnere, lichte Wälder folgen der Straße einige Kilometer weit und lassen sich dann wieder zurückfallen, dunstige Kies-Strände rücken dem Asphaltband auf die Pelle und verabschieden sich dann wieder.

The landscape is breathtakingly beautiful to the left and right of the road: rough mountain massifs rise out of the sea and wander inland, scant forests follow the road for a few kilometers and then disappear again, misty gravel beaches rub shoulders with the asphalt before taking their leave once more.

of our mouths: we have worked out how to embrace the water as part of our journey. You just let yourself drift, allowing the road to find its way. From patience-sapping fjord circuits, leisurely ferries, tunnels under bays and fjords or bridges – we get the feeling things are now starting to pick up pace. The landscape is breathtakingly beautiful to the left and right of the road: rough mountain massifs rise out of the sea and wander inland, scant forests follow the road for a few kilometers and then disappear again, misty gravel beaches rub shoulders with the asphalt before taking their leave once more. The further south we go, to the Lofoten Islands, the more dramatic the spectacle becomes. It is as if nature had considered every few kilometers how to make the trip even more breath-taking.

From Svolvær we take an idyllic drive along European Route 10 to Henningsvær, probably the only place in the world with a football pitch in an island dell. After Leknes we have arrived in the south of the Lofoten archipelago: the island of Moskenesøy is the highlight of this first stage. With its cone-shaped mountains, islands dotted in the sea and deep bays, it feels like a concentrated version of the journey so far. At the spectacularly situated Reine we hop from island to island for one last time until we find ourselves at the port of Moskenes. We've come to the end of the first stage. From here it takes about three hours on the ferry to the mainland. And then onward.

HOTEL

HOLMEN LOFOTEN
E10 3180
8392 SORVÅGEN
WWW.HOLMENLOFOTEN.NO

TROMSØ MOSKENES

Weit im Norden beginnt die Reise: Zwischen Nordkap und Lofoten versteckt sich Tromsø tief in einem Fjord der norwegischen Küste, hier hat man es nicht weit nach Schweden oder Finnland – bis zur norwegischen Hauptstadt Oslo sind es hingegen über 1.600 Kilometer. Das Land rund um Tromsø bietet mit seinen Inseln, Bergen und Meeresarmen einen ersten Vorgeschmack auf den Charakter der kommenden Reise-Etappen. Wir wollen hinüber zu den vorgelagerten Lofoten-Inseln und könnten dafür eine ruhigere Inlandsroute wählen, setzen aber auf die ausgesetztere Variante entlang der Küste. Um hier voranzukommen, müssen alle Register gezogen werden: Brücken und Tunnel führen von Insel zu Insel, langwierige Fjord-Umrundungen werden durch spektakuläre Ausblicke belohnt, immer wieder führen nur noch Fährlinien weiter. Vom Gryllefjord bis zur Insel Andøya ist eine der ersten langen Fährverbindungen zu erwarten und im Süden der Lofoten angekommen wissen wir, dass sich der weite Weg gelohnt hat: Mit andächtig machender Schönheit endet die erste Etappe bei Reine und am Hafen von Moskenes.

—

Our journey begins far in the north: Tromsø is hidden deep in a fjord on the Norwegian coast between the North Cape and Lofoten. It is not far from here to Sweden or Finland, but, on the other hand, it is over 1,600 kilometers to the Norwegian capital, Oslo. The country around Tromsø, with its islands, mountains and inlets, offers a first taste of the upcoming stages of the journey. Our plan is to cross over to the offshore Lofoten Islands and we could choose a quieter inland route to do this, but decide on the more exposed coastal route. In order to make progress here, we need to pull out all the stops: bridges and tunnels lead from island to island; long circuits of fjords are rewarded with spectacular views; time and again ferry services are the only way to continue our trip. We expected one of the first long ferry connections would be from the Gryllefjord to the island of Andøya, and when we arrive in southern Lofoten we know that the long journey was worth it: the first stage ends at Reine and the awe-inspiring beauty of the port of Moskenes.

850 KM • 3-4 TAGE // 530 MILES • 3-4 DAYS

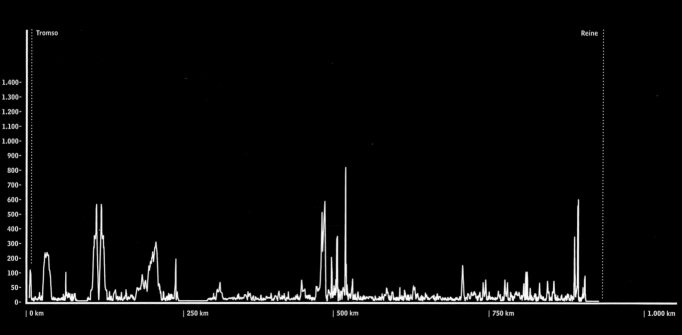

BODØ
ÅLESUND

1.274KM • 3-4 TAGE // 792 MILES • 3-4 DAYS

Stampfend und schäumend schiebt sich die Fähre aus Moskenes in den Hafen von Bodø. Das stählerne Ungetüm vibriert unter unseren Füßen, viele Tausend PS und mächtige Schiffsschrauben lassen das dunkelgrüne Wasser sprudelnd gegen die Mauern des Hafenbeckens schwappen.

—

Pounding against the foaming waves, the ferry powers its way from Moskenes to the port of Bodø. The steel behemoth vibrates under our feet, the thousands of horsepower behind the powerful propellers making the dark green water slap the walls of the harbor basin.

HOTEL

RADISSON BLU HOTEL BODO
STORGATA 2, 8006 BODO
WWW.RADISSONHOTELS.COM

Dann erreicht die Fähre einen Schwebezustand neben dem Kai, Taue fliegen, nehmen das Schiff an die Leine und bevor die Schiffsmaschinen verebben, heben sich bereits die Tore, senkt sich die stählerne Rampe und die ersten Autos rollen aufs feste Land. Auch wir entkommen dem Schiffsrumpf, lassen uns vom Strom der Fahrzeuge vom Hafengelände spülen und stürmen weiter. Nach Osten, weg von der Stadt, dem Verlauf des mächtigen Saltfjorden ins Landesinnere folgend. Der Meeresarm ist von der Europastraße 10 aus kaum zu sehen, versteckt sich am Fuß von weiten Wiesen, hinter Häusern und sanften Hügeln. Erst an seinem Ende lässt er uns an sich heran, wir nehmen hier die Tverlands-Brücke ans Südufer, verschwinden dann aber sofort auf der Fv17 wieder in sichere Distanz. Rollen auf dem felsigen Rücken einer Landzunge nach Süden und können unser Ziel kaum erwarten: Im Landesinneren liegen riesige Fjorde, Skjerstadford und Saltdalsfjord, die bei jeder Flut enorme Wassermassen speichern – und sie bei Ebbe wieder verlieren. Dieser Gezeitenstrom wäre in einer anderen Küstenlandschaft völlig unmerklich, aber hier versperren Inseln den Weg des Wassers, es muss

Finally the ferry comes to a stop next to the quay and ropes are cast hither and tither, taming the vessel. The gates already start to rise before the ship's engines die. The steel ramp drops and the first cars roll onto dry land. We also emerge from the depths of the ship's hull, allowing ourselves to be washed along in the stream of vehicles from the port area, then storming forward. We head east, away from the city, following the course of the mighty Saltfjorden fjord inland. You can barely catch a glimpse of the sea from European Route 10, as it lies hidden at the foot of wide meadows, behind houses and gently rolling hills. Only as we reach the end of the fjord does it let us come closer, as we take the Tverlands Bridge to the south bank, then immediately disappearing back to a safe distance on the Fv17.

We roll south on a rocky headland ridge, impatient to reach our destination: inland lie the huge fjords of Skjerstadford and Saltdalsfjord, which store enormous amounts of water with every high tide before draining again at low tide. This tidal current would go unnoticed in any other coastal landscape, but here islands block the water's

durch schmale Rinnen hinein und hinaus. Das Resultat dieser Flaschenhälse für Millionen Kubikmeter von Meerwasser sind mächtige, furchterregende Mahlströme, in denen dunkelblaues Wasser schäumt, Blasen schlägt und sich immer wieder zu riesigen Strudeln formt. Die Meerwasserströme werden in den schmalen Rinnen des Saltstraumen oder Sundstraumen während der Gezeitengänge zu reißenden Flüssen, teilweise bis zu 30 km/h schnell.

Mit leisem Grusel schauen wir von der Saltstraumenbrücke hinunter ins aufgewühlte Wasser, in dem spiegelglatte Oberflächen aussehen, als würde unter ihnen jeden Moment eine Blase aus Dampf platzen, während sich direkt daneben das Wasser zu türkisgrün schäumenden Sprudelbecken aufbäumt oder in furchterregenden Strudeln dreht. Für Landratten ein beinahe beängstigendes Schauspiel. Und im sonst so idyllischen Umfeld der Küste beinahe unwirklich. Sträucher, Moos und Flechten bedecken die felsigen Inselhügel, Birkenwälder leuchten, in der Ferne ragen schneebedeckte Berge in einen weiten Himmel.

Wir fahren andächtig, die Straße schneidet in die bewaldeten Berghänge der Inseln, dann öffnet sich das Land wieder: Ein Gebirgsbach ist auf dem Weg zum Meer unterwegs, Pools mit glasklarem Wasser füllen sich zwischen Felsen und die Straße steigt auf Zehenspitzen über dieses Diorama hinweg. Weiter, weiter. Zurück in den Birkenwald, zurück ans Ufer des Holmsundfjord, an den sich hier wieder mächtige Gebirgszüge fügen. Lediglich ein schmaler Streifen Land bleibt dem Asphaltband, das unter Steilwänden entlangzieht. Und immer dann, wenn etwas mehr Platz bleibt, haben sich neben der Straße Häuser eingenistet, die uns aus verschlafenen Gardinenaugen hinterherschauen: grauer Sockel, beiges Obergeschoss. Oder Bauernhöfe, getüncht im typischen Rot des Nordens. Falunrot heißt der erdig-dumpfe Farbton, nach einer mittlerweile stillgelegten Kupfermine im schwedischen Falun, von deren Abraumhalden die Pigmente für den auch in Norwegen gern genutzten Anstrich stammten. Kupfer aus Falun gibt es schon einige Jahrzehnte nicht mehr, aber die backsteinrote Farbe ist geblieben. Als dauerndes Erkennungszeichen Skandinaviens.

path, forcing it to enter and exit through narrow gullies. These bottlenecks for millions of cubic meters of seawater cause powerful, terrifying maelstroms in which dark blue water foams, bubbles, and eddies over and over again. The seawater currents in the narrow channels of the Saltstraumen or Sundstraumen become raging torrents as the tide flows in and out, sometimes reaching speeds of up to 30 km/h.

With a slight shudder we gaze down from Saltstraumen Bridge into the turbulent water, in which mirror-smooth areas look as if a bubble of steam is about to burst beneath them, while right next to them the water rears up into turquoise-green foaming spouts or twists in terrifying whirlpools. This is a terrifying spectacle for landlubbers and has an element of the unreal in the otherwise idyllic surroundings of the coast. Shrubs, moss and lichen cover the rocky island hills, birch forests glint, in the distance snow-capped mountains rise toward a wide open sky. We drive on with reverence. The road cuts into the forested mountainsides of the islands, then the land opens up again: a mountain stream makes its way to the sea, pools of crystal clear water form between rocks as we pick our way through this diorama. Onward, ever onward.

Then back to the birch forest and back to the shore of the Holmsundfjord, which once again joins with mighty mountain ranges. Only a narrow strip of land remains for the ribbon of asphalt that curls under the steep rocky walls. Whenever there is space enough, little groups of houses spring up on the side of the road, watching us sleepily from behind the curtains: gray on the bottom, beige up top. These alternate with farmsteads, painted in the typical red of the north. Falun red is the name for the dull, earthy shade. It derives from a now closed copper mine in Falun, Sweden, whose spoil heaps were the source of the pigments for the paint, which is also popular in Norway. Copper from Falun has been gone for several decades, but the brick red color has remained as a permanent identifier of Scandinavian vernacular architecture.

In front of one of the houses, a young man is making circles on a ride-on lawnmower,

HOTEL & RESTAURANT

NORSK HAVBRUKSSENTER - RORBUER
TOFTVEIEN 80
8909 BRONNOYSUND
WWW.HAVBRUKSSENTER.NO

Vor einem Haus zieht ein junger Mann auf dem Rasenmähertraktor Kreise, raspelt den kargen Grasbewuchs stoppelkurz. Er trägt einen Kopfhörer und bangt konzentriert head. Die brachiale Gitarren- und Double-Bass-Breitseite des Metal-Songs, mit dem er sich das Rasenmassaker versüßt, schafft es aber nicht bis zu uns herüber. Wir nicken grüßend, er bangt zurück. Nehmen wir an. Und fahren weiter. Immer weiter, bis wir beim kleinen Ort Storvik das offene Meer erreichen. Aber auch das ist nur ein kurzer Moment, denn schon stellen sich uns wieder Bergriesen in den Weg, zwingen uns zurück ins Labyrinth der Fjorde, in den Rhythmus der Landschaft. Und unter dem Svartisengletscher sogar in einen Tunnel, die pure Klaustrophobie, beinahe 8 Kilometer lang und so eng, dass ein ausgewachsener Troll die Röhre auf dem Bauch liegend durchrobben müsste. Was man jetzt wohl tut, wenn einem auf halbem Weg ein dahinrobbender Troll entgegenkommt? – Ja, das überlegt man sich hier unter dem Berg durchaus und ist seltsam erleichtert, wenn einen das Nadelöhr im Fels auf der anderen Seite wieder ausspuckt.

Am Forøy-Fährkai, einige Kilometer weiter, ist die Troll-im-Tunnel-Überlegung nur noch eine lächerliche Erinnerung, das Land liegt da wie Postkarten-Kitsch und wir vertreten uns auf dem Deck der kleinen Fähre hinüber nach Ågskardet die Beine. Knapp dreißig Kilometer später haben wir bereits die nächste Fähre erreicht, genau rechtzeitig für einen Hotdog an Bord, das inoffizielle Lieblingsgericht aller Fährleute. Innerhalb einer Dreiviertelstunde zieht der Pott gelassen von Jektvik bis Kilboghavn, das reicht sogar für zwei Hotdogs. Und einen Kaffee. Und einen immer tieferen Ruhepuls. Gemessen in Beats-per-Minute ist dies wohl die gelassenste aller CURVES-Reisen, irgendwann ertappen wir uns beim 60-km/h-Dahinschlendern sogar mit Country-and-Western-Songs im Satellitenradio. Gepflegte innere Einkehr, während hinter der Windschutzscheibe eine spektakuläre Landschafts-Doku abrollt. Stunde um Stunde. Norwegen ist groß, Norwegen ist sperrig, Norwegen ist langsam. Berge, Fjorde, Fähren, Hot Dogs und Kaffee. Wir streunen durch Mo i Rana, landen bei Tjøtta wieder weit draußen im Reich der Schäreninseln und danach beim kleinen Weiler Kongsmoen

rasping the sparse grass to stubble. He's wearing headphones and bobbing his head in concentration. We can't hear the brutish guitar and double-bass broadside of the heavy metal song that acts as a soundtrack to this lawn massacre. We nod our greeting, which he seems to return. We then drive onward until we reach the open sea at a little place called Storvik.

But even that is only for a brief moment, because the mountain giants block our way again, forcing us back into the labyrinth of the fjords and the rhythm of the landscape. And even in a tunnel under the Svartisen glacier, pure claustrophobia, almost 8 kilometers long and so constricted that a full-grown troll would have to crawl through on his stomach. What would you do now if a troll were to come crawling to meet you halfway? – All of these things go through your mind as you pass under the mountain, feeling strangely relieved when the narrow split in the rock disgorges you on the other side.

At the Forøy ferry port, a few kilometers further on, the troll-in-the-tunnel idea is just a ridiculous memory. The landscape is spread before us in picture-postcard kitsch as we stretch our legs on the deck of the small ferry across to Ågskardet. Barely thirty kilometers later, we have already reached the next ferry, just in time for a hot dog on board, the unofficial favorite dish of all ferry users. Within three quarters of an hour, the behemoth moves in stately fashion from Jektvik to Kilboghavn. Plenty of time for two hot dogs. And a coffee. And an ever lower resting heart rate. Measured in beats per minute, this is probably the most relaxed CURVES journey ever. At one point we even catch ourselves cruising along at 60 km/h with country and western songs on satellite radio. An air of cultivated contemplation descends while hour after hour of a spectacular landscape documentary plays just beyond the windshield.

Norway is a big, awkwardly shaped country, a place where life is lived in the slow lane. Mountains, fjords, ferries, hot dogs and coffee. We pass through Mo i Rana, end up at a far point on the archipelago at Tjøtta and then at the small hamlet of Kongsmoen

HOTELS & RESTAURANTS

BRITANNIA HOTEL & SPEILSALEN
DRONNINGENSGATE 5
7011 TRONDHEIM
WWW.BRITANNIA.NO

FAGN
ORJAVEITA 4
7010 TRONDHEIM
WWW.FAGN.NO

SUSHI BAR
MUNKEGATA 41
7011 TRONDHEIM
WWW.SUSHIBAR.NO

am Ende des Folda-Fjords, das beinahe 90 Kilometer vom offenen Meer entfernt ist. Staunen, wundern, fahren. Bis Trondheim. Als wir an der Stadt vorbeirollen, wissen wir nicht, ob die letzten 900 Kilometer nun innerhalb eines Wimpernschlags vorbeigezogen sind, innerhalb von Tagen oder während eines Menschenlebens. Wir verpassen den richtigen Moment für das Ende dieser Mammut-Etappe, lassen das Segel des Drachenboots weiter im Wind, wir ziehen auf der E 39 nach Südwesten. Mit Ziel Kristiansund.

Hier haben wir den finalen Tusch dieser Etappe erreicht, das Crescendo. Wir tauchen hinter der Stadt in den Tunnel der Atlantikstraße, der steil zum Meeresgrund hinabführt, sich unter Seewasser und Schlick in den Fels gräbt. Lichter ziehen vorbei, rhythmisch, wie Futter für Pac-Man, dann ist die tiefste Stelle in einer Kammer erreicht und die Röhre steigt wieder hinauf. Drüben, im Tageslicht, streunt die Straße über die flechtenbedeckten Felsen der Insel Averøya. Die schichten sich hier schräg in die Erdkruste, als Blätterteig aus Stein, glattgehobelt von Eiszeit-Gletschern, und nur in den Senken hat sich eine dünne Erdschicht angesammelt, auf der karge Wiesen und struppiges Gehölz stehen. Zwischen Teichen und Seen schlingert die Straße dahin, und an ihrem nordwestlichen Ende geht es los: Im Dreisprung hechtet der „Atlanterhavsveien" von Insel zu Insel, swingt dahin, schiebt seine Trasse zwischen Felsen, quert auf Deichen und Dämmen und segelt dann in einer eleganten Aufwärts-Seitwärts-Bewegung über die Storseisundsbrücke. Richtungswechsel am höchsten Punkt der Brücke – da hört man die Planer und Straßenbauer immer noch lachen, vor Vergnügen.

Bis Molde haben wir uns von der unwirklichen Anmut dieses Moments wieder erholt, immer noch schmunzelnd rollen wir auf die Fähre hinüber nach Vestnes und jetzt sind es noch 65 Kilometer bis ans Ende dieser langen, raumgreifenden Etappe. Bodø nach Ålesund, das ist episch. Weit. Ermüdend. Erquickend. 1.000 Kilometer voller Schönheit, Fahren in Trance. Und jetzt sind wir hier. Sitzen am Hafen von Ålesund und schauen aufs Meer hinaus, während Schiffe im unwirklichen Schein der Mitternachtssonne aus leuchtendem Dunst auftauchen. Das vergisst du nie wieder.

at the end of the Folda fjord, almost 90 kilometers from the open sea. We stop to marvel and drive on in wonder as far as Trondheim. As we roll past the city, we're unsure whether the last 900 kilometers have passed in the blink of an eye, in days or in a lifetime. We miss the right moment for the end of this mammoth stage and leave the sail of the Viking longboat flying in the wind, as we head south-west on the E39, destination Kristiansund.

Here we have reached the final flourish of this stage, the crescendo. Beyond the city we plunge deep into the tunnel of the Atlantic Road, which descends steeply to the seabed, digging into the rock under seawater and silt. Lights flash past rhythmically, like fodder for Pac-Man. We reach the deepest point then feel ourselves rising again. On the other side, in bright daylight, the road strays across the lichen-covered rocks of Averøya Island. They are layered here diagonally in the earth's crust, like puff pastry made of stone, ground smooth by Ice Age glaciers, and only in the depressions has a thin layer of earth accumulated, home to barren meadows and scrubby woodland.

The road winds between ponds and lakes, and things really take off at its north-western end: in a triple jump, the "Atlanterhavsveien" Atlantic road dives from island to island, swinging along, pushing its way between rocks, crossing dikes and dams and then sails in an elegant sideways and upward movement over the Storseisund Bridge. As it changes direction at the highest point, you can almost hear the engineers and road builders laughing with delight.

By the time we reach Molde we have recovered from the unreal grace of this moment. Still smiling we roll onto the ferry over to Vestnes and now we still have 65 kilometers to go to the end of this long, extensive stage. The section from Bodø to Ålesund is truly epic. This has been a long, tiring, refreshing 1,000 kilometers of beauty. It feels like we've been driving in a trance. And suddenly we've arrived. Sitting by the harbor in Ålesund and looking out to sea as ships emerge from the glowing haze in the surreal glow of the midnight sun – a sight you'll never forget.

HOTELS

SAGA FJORD HOTEL
OYRAGATA 8, 6165 SAEBO
WWW.SAGAFJORDHOTEL.NO

HOTEL BROSUNDET
APOTEKERGATA 1-5,
6004 ÅLESUND
WWW.BROSUNDET.NO

STORFJORD HOTEL
OVRE GLOMSET
SKODJE
WWW.STORFJORDHOTEL.COM

BODØ ÅLESUND

Mit der Mammut-Etappe von Bødo bis Ålesund schlagen wir einen über 1.000 Kilometer weiten Bogen vom Tor zu den Lofoten bis in den Südwesten Norwegens. Von jenseits des Polarkreises bis zu den majestätischen Fjorden. Und zugegeben: Es gibt Momente auf dieser Fahrt, in denen man sich wünscht, schon angekommen zu sein, einfach weil der Weg so weit ist. Und Norwegen macht es einem nicht leicht: Im Labyrinth der Inseln und Meeresarme zählt jeder Kilometer doppelt. Und trotzdem bereuen wir die hier verbrachten Stunden nicht: Die leuchtende Schönheit der norwegischen Atlantik-Küste wird niemals zur Wiederholung, der Spannungsbogen bricht nicht. Handfeste Gründe auf diese „Reise in der Reise" zu gehen, gibt es durchaus: Nur so lassen sich die Lofoten auf Achse erleben. Wer dort oben sein und nicht fliegen möchte, muss fahren. Und die Mahlströme rund um den Saltfjorden sind für sich allein eine Reise wert. Das unaufhörliche Fähren-und-Insel-Hopping entlang der Küstenlinie ebenfalls. Es entsteht ein eigentümlicher Groove aus Fahren und Warten, der einen geduldig und demütig macht, das muss man erlebt haben. Trondheim dürfte für fortgeschrittene Norwegen-Fahrer ebenfalls eine Reise wert sein. Und wenn man dann nach Kristiansund am Atlanterhavsveien ankommt, ist das wie eine Verheißung auf kommende Abenteuer, die den zurückliegenden Kilometern Sinn geben und den kommenden Glanz. Wir würden es immer wieder tun. Weil es sein muss.

—

The mammoth stage from Bødo to Ålesund covers a 1,000-kilometer arc from the gateway to the Lofoten Islands to the south-west of Norway. We travel from beyond the Arctic Circle to the majestic fjords. Admittedly there are moments on this trip when you wish were already at your destination, simply because it is such a long way. Also, Norway doesn't make things easy: in the labyrinth of islands and inlets, every kilometer counts twice. And yet we don't regret the hours we spent here: the radiant beauty of the Norwegian Atlantic coast is never to be repeated, the suspense never breaks. There are plenty of good reasons to go on this "journey within a journey": this is the only way to experience Lofoten Islands on the move. If you want get there without flying, you have to drive. The maelstroms around the Saltfjorden are enough on their own to take the trip worthwhile. The same goes for the endless ferries and island hopping along the coastline. You get into a peculiar groove of driving and waiting, which makes you patient and humble – something you have to experience to understand. Trondheim should also be worth a trip for advanced Norway drivers. And then when you arrive at Atlanterhavsveien after Kristiansund, it's like a promise of adventures to come, making sense of the distance covered and the brilliance to come. We would do it all again and again. After all, it would be a pity not to.

1.274KM • 3-4 TAGE // 792 MILES • 3-4 DAYS

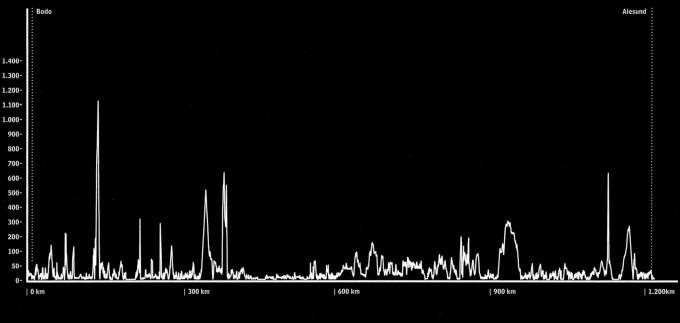

STAVBERGVATNET

ÅLESUND LÆRDAL

750 KM • 2-3 TAGE // 466 MILES • 2-3 DAYS

Im Inneren des Heissafjorden, geschützt durch eine vorgelagerte Insel, liegt Ålesund. Rund um den Hafen sammeln sich wuchtige Steinhäuser, Gassen wandern die umgebenden Hügel hinauf, auf der anderen Seite des Hafenbeckens reihen sich weiße Holzhäuser direkt am Ufer. Alte Fischerkähne zerren an ihren Tauen, während sich moderne Fährschiffe aus dem Dunst des offenen Meers ins ruhige Wasser des Hafens schieben.

—

Inside the Heissafjorden fjord, protected by an outlying island, lies Ålesund. Solid stone houses gather around the harbor, narrow lanes meander up the surrounding hills and on the other side of the bay there are serried ranks of white timber houses right on the water's edge. Old fishing boats tug on their ropes while modern ferries plough their way out of the hazy open sea and into the calm waters of the harbor.

STAVBERGVATNET

GEIRANGERFJORD

ROAD 63 TO TROLLSTIGEN

TROLLSTIGEN

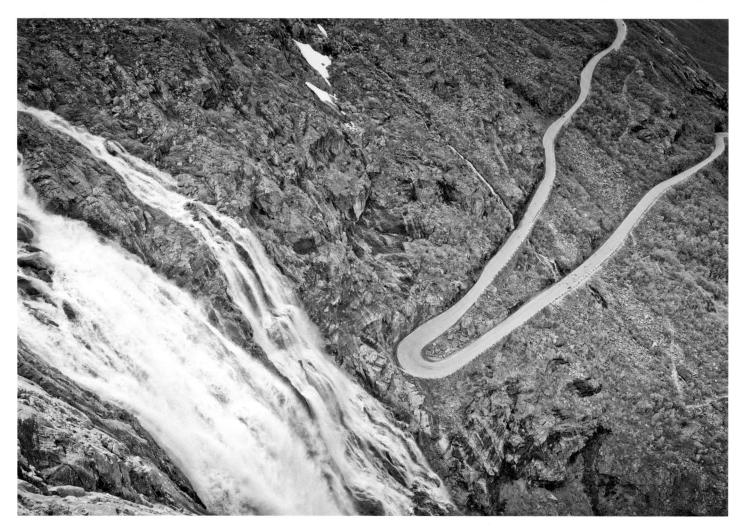

HOTELS

HOTEL UNION OYE
NORANGDAL 41,
6196 NORANGSFJORDEN
WWW.UNIONOYE.NO/NO

RESTAURANT

BRASSERIE POSTEN
GEIRANGERVEGEN 4
6216 GEIRANGER
WWW.BRASSERIEPOSTEN.NO

Die geschäftigen Ausfallstraßen mit ihren Industriebetrieben und Werkstätten sind beinahe ein Schock für uns: So viel Leben nach den vielen, stetigen Kilometern aus dem Norden herunter.

Aber die dritte Etappe zieht uns erneut magisch hinaus, heute werden wir Könige sein. Und das beginnt mit nassen Füßen: Bereits nach wenigen Kilometern wartet die erste Fähre auf uns, auf der E39-Route nach Süden gibt es keinen anderen Weg über den Sulesund. Schon auf der anderen Seite lassen wir die breite Europastraße ohne uns weiterziehen, wir folgen auf Zehenspitzen dem schmalen „Fylkesveg 70" hinein in den Hjørundfjord. Struppige Bergwälder greifen nach dem schmalen Asphaltband, das sich vorsichtig ein paar Meter über der Wasseroberfläche des Fjords dahintastet. Kreisrunde Unterwassergehege für Lachse sammeln sich im grünen Wasser. Je weiter die Straße rollt, desto schwieriger macht es ihr der Fjord: Nur wenige Meter sind zwischen Berg und Wasser für die schmale Trasse geeignet, immer wieder muss sie sich tapfer in den Berg fressen oder gar über aufgeschüttete Damm-Passagen vorwärtskommen – man ahnt, dass das nicht lange so weitergehen wird. Voraus ragt ein mächtiger Berg auf, kantig und grob, Wasserbäche stürzen von seinen Felswänden auf den darunterliegenden steilen Sockel und dieses Ungetüm wird uns nicht vorbeilassen.

Deshalb wechseln wir einfach die Seite, spielen Fjordsurfing über Bande: vom Westufer beim kleinen Weiler Standal per Fähre ans Ostufer bei Trandal, hier aufs nächste Boot in Richtung Sæbø, zurück ans Westufer. Erneut heißt es warten und dann schäumt die nächste Fähre heran, nach Leknes – am Ostufer. Könnte man alles auch in einem Zug von Standal nach Leknes machen, aber wir sind in Abenteuerlaune. Schnüffeln in den kleinen Tälern rechts und links des Fjords nach Schönheiten, folgen kurvigen Straßen in die oberen Stockwerke der mächtigen Massive entlang des Meeresarms – und haben eine Verabredung. Auf einem kleinen Flugplatz wartet unsere Maschine, viersitzig, luftig, verwegen. Mit kernigem Röhren sprintet sie die Startbahn hinunter und hievt sich

The busy arterial roads with their industrial plants and workshops almost come as a shock to us: so much life after the long, steady journey down from the north. But the third stage of our trip entices us onward as if by magic.

Today we can expect to make a royal progress. We start by getting our feet wet: after just a few kilometers, the first ferry is waiting for us, as there is no other way across the Sulesund on the E39 route south. On reaching the other side, we let the wide Euro Route carry on without us, instead tiptoeing into the Hjørundfjord via the narrow "Fylkesveg 70" national route. Scant mountain forests reach toward the narrow ribbon of asphalt that carefully feels its way just a few meters above the watery surface of the fjord. Circular underwater cages for salmon group together in the green water. The further the road goes on, the more difficult it becomes because of the fjord: there are only a few meters between the mountain and the water available for the narrow route, so again and again it has to bravely cut a way through the mountain or even break free to cross dams made of rough boulders. You get the feeling that this arrangement won't last long. The rough outline of a mighty mountain looms ahead, streams of water tumbling from its rock walls onto the steep base below, refusing to allow us to pass.

Our response is simply to switch to the other side of the fjord in a cheeky surfing maneuver: we take the ferry from the west bank at the small hamlet of Standal to the east bank at Trandal, then on the next boat in the direction of Sæbø, back to the west bank again. Again we have to wait a while before the next ferry churns its way up to Leknes – on the east bank. You could do the whole journey on a single train from Standal to Leknes, but we're feeling adventurous. We poke about the small valleys to the right and left of the fjord in search of natural beauty, following winding roads to the upper parts of the mighty massifs along the estuary – after all we have an appointment to keep. A plucky four-seater aircraft awaits us on a small airfield. With a hearty roar, it sprints down the runway and then heaves itself up in a single movement: the valley drops away beneath us and all around us

DJUPEVATN

dann in einem einzigen Schwung empor: Das Tal stürzt unter uns in die Tiefe, ringsum bäumen sich brachiale Bergrücken auf. Mit eng und präzise gezirkelten Bögen manövriert sich das Flugzeug im Tal hinauf, bis es über den Gipfeln angekommen ist. Und jetzt wird alles ganz ruhig: Der eben noch hart hämmernde Motor atmet langsam und ruhig, der Propeller dreht langsamer. Die Fall- und Scherwinde im Tal, die der kleinen Maschine eben noch zugesetzt, sie unruhig hin- und hergeworfen haben, sind verschwunden.

Ringsum breitet sich ein sprachlos machendes Panorama aus: epische Bergrücken, dicht an dicht gepackt, mit Schnee bedeckt, derb und felsig, auf grünem Sockel. Und dazwischen schwarzes Wasser, das in der Sonne glänzt und als Labyrinth in eine Ferne reicht, in der man glasigen Dunst über dem Nordatlantik ahnen kann. Es ist ruhig in den Kopfhörern, niemand spricht, nur das Funkgerät knistert und knackt in den Ohrmuscheln. – Als wir uns viel später wieder am Ufer des Norangsfjord nach Osten tasten und dann in einem wild bewachsenen Tal unter Felshängen ins Landesinnere hineinfahren, sehen wir diese Welt mit völlig anderen Augen.

In Hellesylt ist es wieder so weit: Hier sind wir am Tor zum Geirangerfjord angekommen, in einer Welt des Wassers, und auch hier bringt uns nur eine Fähre weiter. Ins Landesinnere. Straßen haben in diesem Universum für Trolle und Bergriesen keine Chance. Beinahe schwerelos zieht das große Schiff dahin, frisst sich mit dem Bug in einen dunklen Spiegel hinein und hinterlässt eine schäumende Spur. Wasserfälle stürzen aus den Berghängen in den Fjord, Felswände fallen senkrecht in die Tiefe und setzen sich bis weit unter die Wasseroberfläche genau so fort, während mit Schnee bedeckte Gipfel das dramatische Treiben tief unter ihnen beargwöhnen. In einem weiten S-Bogen schwingt der Fjord nach Osten, dann verebbt er in Geiranger. Ein Hurtigruten-Postschiff liegt im Wasser, sanfte Grasmatten steigen aus dem Fjord und erklimmen das Tal hinter dem Ort. Auch eine Straße strebt hier eifrig davon, scheint fest davon überzeugt, uns gleich mitzunehmen, aber wir haben andere

are towering mountain ridges. Performing narrow and precisely curved arcs, the plane maneuvers its way up the valley until it is floating above the peaks. Suddenly everything becomes very quiet: the engine, previously pounding hard, breathes evenly and calmly, the propeller slows. The downdrafts and piercing winds in the valley, which were buffeting the little aircraft just a moment ago, have abated. A breathtaking panorama spreads out around us: epic mountain ridges, densely packed, covered with snow, rough and rocky, on a verdant base. In between, black water glitters in the sun, stretching out in a labyrinthine pattern into the distance, where you can sense a glassy haze hanging over the North Atlantic. Things have gone quiet in the headphones, nobody speaks and all we can hear is the crackle of the radio in our ears. Much later, as we wind our way east again along the shore of the Norangsfjord and then drive inland under rocky slopes in an untamed overgrown valley, we see this world through completely different eyes.

In Hellesylt we arrive at the gateway to the Geirangerfjord, a watery world where once again our only choice if we want to push onward is to board a ferry. We journey inland. The roads in this universe are no place for trolls or mountain giants. The huge vessel glides along almost weightlessly, its bow cleaving the dark mirror of the water and leaving a foaming trail in its wake. Waterfalls cascade from the mountainsides into the fjord, cliff faces plummet vertiginously, continuing well below the waterline, while snow-capped peaks hold themselves aloof from the drama far below. The fjord sweeps east in a wide arcing flourish, ending in Geiringer. A mail boat from the Hurtigruten shipping line lies at anchor. Soft, grassy mats rise from the fjord and climb the valley behind the town. A road leads eagerly away from here, seemingly anxious to take us with it. However, we have other plans. This stage comprises constant detours, an unfathomably capricious journey through the countryside. We cross to the north shore of the fjord, where we pick up another route, spiraling upwards energetically. We are reminded of our previous plane ride as we daringly surf along the mountainside, before swinging upward determinedly. The

HOTEL & RESTAURANT

JUVET LANDSCAPE HOTEL
ALSTAD 24
6210 VALLDAL
WWW.JUVET.COM

GROTLI HOYFJELLSHOTELL
SKJÅKVEGEN 5417
2695 GROTLI
WWW.GROTLI.NO

PRESTESTEINNSVATNET

Pläne. Dies ist eine Etappe der Umwege, ein Irrlichtern durchs Land. Zum Nordufer des Fjords geht es, denn dort nimmt eine andere Route Anlauf, schraubt sich energisch in die Höhe. Beinahe wie vorhin mit dem Flugzeug: waghalsiges Entlangsurfen am Berg, dann entschlossenes Hinaufstürmen. Schon liegt der Fjord tief unter uns, gerade schiebt sich zeitlupenlangsam zögernd ein mächtiges Kreuzfahrtschiff ins Tal, viele Stockwerke hoch. Wir streben über die „Adlerstraße" weiter hinauf, lassen dann die steilen Hänge am Fjord zurück. Immer flacher wird das nach Norden ausgreifende Hochtal, irgendwann ist der gähnende Abgrund hinter uns nur noch eine schillernde Erinnerung.

Hochschalten, Fahrt aufnehmen, dahinströmen, wir fahren mit allen Antennen auf Empfang. Bis zum Norddalsfjord, am anderen Ufer erneut zurück ins obere Stockwerk der Berge und wieder tapsen wir in einem kargen Land dahin: Felsen und Moos, Flechten und schütteres Gras, begleitet von Felsrücken, an denen Wolkenfetzen kleben. So lange, bis die Straße zuerst unmerklich, dann immer stärker nach unten führt. Zwei

fjord is already far below us, and a towering cruise ship is slowly, hesitantly making its way up the valley. We push on up the "Eagle Road", leaving the steep slopes of the fjord behind. The high valley stretching out to the north levels out and at some point the yawning abyss behind us becomes just a shimmering memory. We move up a gear, pick up speed, hitting our stride as we drive on, our antennas tuned to pick up every signal.

We drive as far as the Norddalsfjord, switching back to higher mountain ground on the opposite bank, and again make our way through barren country: rocks and moss, lichen and sparse grass against a backdrop of rocky ridges to which wispy clouds cling. The route continues with the road dipping imperceptibly at first, then following an increasing downward slope. Two mighty mountain peaks form a gateway and the road dives down between them in erratic lurching movements, flashing past a mountain lake. From this point onward there is no holding back: the world falls away, gray-black titanic rock faces open up a broad vista and far below an unbelievably expansive lush green valley comes into view. It must be beautiful down

AURLANDSVEGEN

mächtige Bergzinnen bilden ein Tor und die Straße sackt dazwischen in fahrigen Schlingerbewegungen hinunter, saust an einem Gebirgssee vorbei und ab dann gibt es kein Halten mehr: Die Welt sackt weg, grauschwarze Felswand-Titanen öffnen einen weiten Raum und tief unten schiebt sich in unfassbarer Weite ein sattgrünes Tal heran. Es muss schön sein dort unten, aber der einzige Weg in die Tiefe führt über ein Ungetüm von Serpentinenstraße – wir sind am Trollstigen angelangt. Der Leiter für Trolle. Und natürlich steigen wir auf ihr nach unten. Nur, um danach wieder hinaufzufahren, ungläubig den Kopf schüttelnd über dieses Monument aus Kurven im Fels. Man muss hier gewesen sein.

Aber das gilt für so vieles auf dieser Etappe. Nicht einmal der weite Rückweg zum Geirangerfjord ist langweilig, die spektakuläre Route über den Dalsnibba-Pass eine Legende, die Wege in den Flusstälern von Otta, Bøvra und Leira pure Schönheit. Und bevor wir das Ziel der Etappe rund um Lærdal erreichen, geht es schließlich noch einmal ganz hoch hinaus. Aus lieblichen Tälern voller Grün und gelassen dahinplätschernder Flüsse bis unter einen majestätischen Himmel, dem nur die Felsgiganten des Inlandsgebirges auf Augenhöhe begegnen. Überlebensgroße Cinemascope-Eindrücke sammeln wir auf der Route über Erdal zum Vedahaugane und den Aurlandsfjellet zum Stegastein. Für den Rückweg nach Lærdal nehmen wir den Tunnel der Europastraße 16 und selbst der hat hier Lust auf gute Unterhaltung: Mitten in der Röhre öffnet sich eine Kuppel im Fels, die Decke ist mysteriös blau beleuchtet, die rohen Felswände werden grün und ocker angestrahlt. Innerhalb von Sekunden huschen wir durch diesen bizarren Moment, dann setzt sich das Dunkel des Lærdal-Tunnels ungerührt fort. Als wäre nichts gewesen.

Einige Minuten später sitzen wir dann in der Stabkirche von Borgund und lassen unsere Synapsen die Bilder und Eindrücke dieses Tags verdauen. Langsam, ganz langsam berühren unsere Füße wieder den Boden. Touchdown. Landung. Aber ein kleines Irrlicht der Seele wird wohl für immer da oben durch die Berge Norwegens streifen.

> **Nicht einmal der weite Rückweg zum Geirangerfjord ist langweilig, die spektakuläre Route über den Dalsnibba-Pass eine Legende, die Wege in den Flusstälern von Otta, Bøvra und Leira pure Schönheit.**

> Not even the long return journey to the Geirangerfjord is boring. The spectacular route over the Dalsnibba Pass is legendary, while the sections in the river valleys of Otta, Bøvra and Leira are spectacularly beautiful.

there, but the only way down is via an endless series of switchbacks. Finally we arrive at Trollstigen, the troll's ladder. Naturally we descend on it, only to climb back up afterwards, shaking our heads in disbelief at this monument to rocky curves. This is a place has to be seen to be believed.

But the same could be said of much of this stage of our trip. Not even the long return journey to the Geirangerfjord is boring. The spectacular route over the Dalsnibba Pass is legendary, while the sections in the river valleys of Otta, Bøvra and Leira are spectacularly beautiful. Before we reach the end of the stage at Lærdal, we have one last climb from lovely valleys full of lush greenery and serenely babbling brooks to a majestic sky road that only the rocky giants of the inland mountains meet at eye level. We absorb larger than life cinemascope-style impressions on the route via Erdal to Vedahaugane and the Aurlandsfjellet to Stegastein. Making our way back to Lærdal, we take the tunnel of European Route 16, which is also in the mood to provide some good entertainment: in the middle of the tunnel a dome opens up in the rock, the ceiling is lit in a mysterious blue, while the raw rock walls are illuminated in green and ocher. We pass through this bizarre scene in a matter of seconds, before plunging back into the darkness of the Lærdal Tunnel as if nothing had happened. A few minutes later we find ourselves sitting in the Borgund stave church, letting our synapses absorb the images and impressions of the day. Slowly, very slowly, our feet touch the ground again. Touchdown. Landing. But a little part of our souls will probably roam the mountains of Norway forever.

HOTEL & RESTAURANT

LAERDALSOREN GUESTHOUSE
OYRAGATA 15, 6887 LAERDAL
WWW.LARDALSORENHOTEL.NO

BRYGGEHUSET
FV338 8
6879 SOLVORN

ÅLESUND LÆRDAL

Aus Ålesund kommt man nur in Richtung Süden weiter, wenn man die Fähre nimmt, und das wird für die ersten Kilometer dieser Etappe ein prägendes Element bleiben: Unterwegs im Hjørundfjord, einem Seitenarm des weltberühmten Geirangerfjords, führt die Straße nur ungefähr bis zur Hälfte, ab dann geht es nur auf dem Schiff weiter. Der Geirangerfjord schiebt sich derweil nördlich durch die Berge, bei Hellesylt haben wir ihn nach einer Überquerung des dazwischenliegenden Bergkamms erreicht, und auch er macht ein Vorankommen auf der Straße unmöglich: Nur per Fähre kann man Geiranger von Westen her erreichen. Über die sogenannte Adlerstraße verlassen wir den Fjord nach Norden, wechseln zum Tafjord und fahren dann über den Valldal-Nationalpark zum Trollstigen. Die spektakuläre Serpentinenstraße ist hier das Tor zum Romsdalsfjord bei Åndalsnes. Unsere Route führt aber zurück nach Geiranger, und von dort über den Dalsnibba-Pass nach Südosten, hinaus aus der Provinz Møre og Romsdal, über einen Abschnitt durch Innlandet in die Provinz Vestland. Am Lærdalsfjord haben wir das Ziel der Etappe beinahe erreicht, schließen aber noch zwei Entdeckungsreisen zum Stegastein-Aussichtspunkt und ins nahe gelegene Borgund-Tal an.

—

The only way south from Ålesund is to take the ferry. This will remain a defining element for the first few kilometers of this stage: as we travel along the Hjørundfjord, a side arm of the world-famous Geirangerfjord, the road only takes you half way before you have to transfer to ship. The Geirangerfjord meanwhile pushes north through the mountains. We reach it at Hellesylt, having crossed the intervening ridge, and find it impossible to go any further by road: Geiranger can only be reached from the west by ferry. We leave the fjord to the north via the so-called Eagle Road, switching to the Tafjord and then driving via the Valldal National Park to the Trollstigen. The spectacular serpentine road here is the gateway to the Romsdalsfjord at Åndalsnes. However, our route takes us back to Geiranger, and from there over the Dalsnibba pass southeast, out of Møre og Romsdal province, via a section through Innlandet into Vestland province. Arriving at the Lærdalsfjord we have almost reached the final destination of this stage, although two journeys of discovery still await us: the Stegastein lookout point and the nearby Borgund Valley.

750 KM • 2-3 TAGE // 466 MILES • 2-3 DAYS

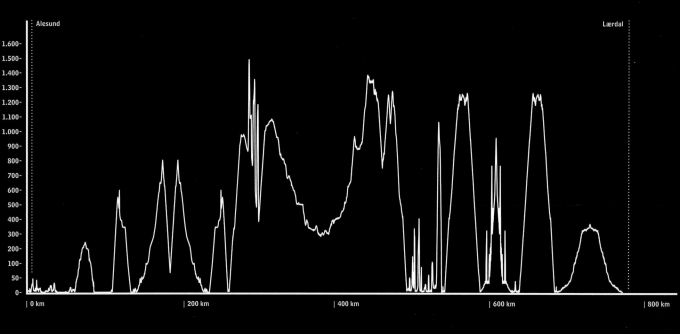

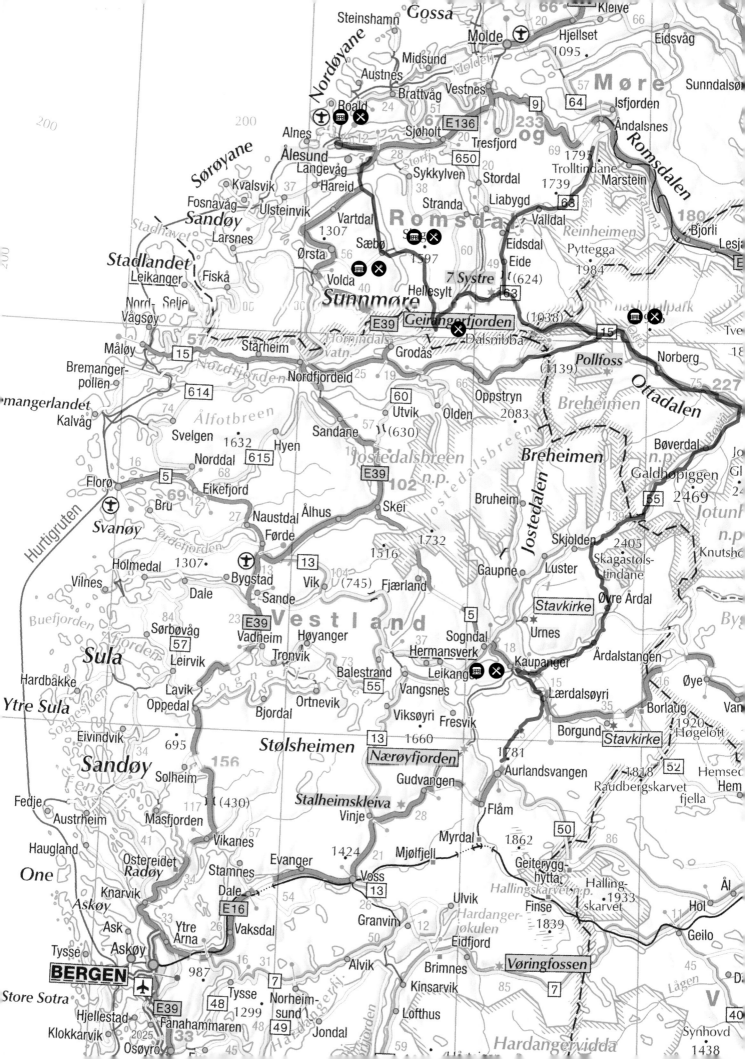

STABKIRCHE BORGUND

LÆRDAL
STAVANGER

890 KM • 2-3 TAGE // 553 MILES • 2-3 DAYS

Guten Tag, sagt der Fodnestunnel hinter Lærdal, er bleckt die Zähne und dann verschwinden wir in seinem Schlund. Allzu lang dauert die Fahrt durch die Eingeweide des Bergs am Sognefjord aber nicht, und auch die Fähre zwischen Fodnes und Mannheller geht uns mittlerweile locker von der Hand: Hop on, hop off und weiter geht's.

—

The Fodnes Tunnel greets us beyond Lærdal, baring its teeth as we disappear into its gullet. The journey through the bowels of the mountain on the Sognefjord doesn't take long, and the ferry between Fodnes and Mannheller is now no problem for us seasoned seadogs: we hop on and off, and on we go.

BØYABREEN

HOTEL

RIVERSIDE FARM LODGE
TOKVAMSVEGEN 12
5745 AURLAND
WWW.292AURLAND.COM

TROLLTUNGA APARTMENTS VIKING HAUG
HOVDEN 15
5750 ODDA
WWW.VIKINGHAUG.NO

Vorbei an der Stabkirche von Kaupanger, die streng und düster zwischen Grabsteinen im Tal thront, ausgespien von einem Zeitreise-Tunnel aus anderen Sphären. Rüber nach Sogndal und dann im Tal der Sogndalselvi nach Norden. So beginnt unsere Reise nach Stavanger.

Der kleine Fluss wird nach wenigen Kilometern zu einem See, träumt dunkelgrün und mit spiegelglatter Oberfläche von einem geruhsamen Leben, aber dann geht es doch wieder eilig weiter. Die Straße macht nun gewaltig Fahrt, fackelt nicht lange mit den Bergen, die sich ihr entgegenrüpeln, und hämmert als Frudalstunnel mitten hindurch. Taucht kurz beim Einbiegen in den Fjærlandsfjord zum Luftholen auf und segelt dann weiter unter der Erdoberfläche nach Norden. Erst am Ende des Fjærlandsfjords holen wir das Segel ein und lassen uns ins Tal hineintreiben, auf einen Stopp am Gletschermuseum. Dichter und dramatischer als hier lässt sich die Geschichte dieser Landschaft kaum erkennen: Tal und Fjord sind Reste der Eiszeit und oben auf dem Berg leuchten noch schneeweiß die Reste der Gletscher. Als Jostedaalsbreen hat sich hier eine mächtige Eishaube auf den Zinnen des Gebirges gehalten, der Gletscher wehrt sich nach Leibeskräften, wird aber als Kollateralschaden des Klimawandels unaufhörlich abgetaut. Die zwei Zungen des Bøyabreen und Flatbreen ziehen sich hier unten immer weiter zurück.

Wir stehen auf dem Grund des Tals, am Rand einer Schmelzwasserlache, und legen den Kopf in den Nacken: Früher hat sich der Gletscher noch bis ins Tal gedrängt, jetzt lugt er oben misstrauisch über den Rand einer Felskante und wirft ab und zu Eisbrocken herunter. Die fallen ins Wasser, treiben dort eine Weile und lösen sich dann auf. Einen der leuchtenden Klumpen lassen wir in der Hand schmelzen und denken, sonderbar berührt, dass sich da gerade Schnee aus der Wikingerzeit in unserer Hand zu Wasser verwandelt. Und dass auch die kleinen Bläschen im Eis mit Luft von damals gefüllt sind. Sonderbar. Und traurig irgendwie ... Im Fjærlandstunnel finden wir einen Weg unter dem Eispanzer hindurch, landen am Jøstravatnet - und

We pass the Kaupanger stave church, which sits sternly and somberly enthroned between gravestones in the valley, spat out by a time tunnel from another world. Over to Sogndal and then northward in the valley of the Sogndalselvi. Our journey to Stavanger has begun.

After a few kilometers the little river becomes a lake with a dark green, mirror-smooth surface, evoking dreams of a peaceful life, but soon hurries on again. The road picks up speed, dispensing quickly with the mountains that loom toward it, and instead powering its way through the middle in the guise of the Frudals Tunnel. It comes up briefly for air as you turn toward the Fjærlandsfjord, then sallies further north underground. We only slow down at the end of Fjærlandsfjord and drift down into the valley, stopping at the Glacier Museum. The history of this landscape can hardly be witnessed with greater intensity and drama than here: the valley and fjord are remnants of the ice age and the last of the glacier still shines snowy white on the mountain summit.

A mighty cap of ice has held onto the peaks of the mountains here in the form of the Jostedaalsbreen glacier, which is fighting a losing battle with constant thaw as collateral damage from climate change. The two tongues of the Bøyabreen and Flatbreen glaciers are retreating further and further down here. We stand at the bottom of the valley, at the edge of a pool of melt water, and turn our gaze upward: the glacier used to push its way down into the valley, but now it peers suspiciously over the edge of a cliff, occasionally throwing down chunks of ice. They fall into the water, float there for a while and then dissolve. We let some of the pure white mass melt in our hands and consider that snow from the Viking era is turning to water before our eyes. Also that the tiny bubbles in the ice are filled with air from the same time. These are strangely touching thoughts, as well as somehow kind of sad...

The Fjærlands Tunnel provides us with a way under the ice sheet, ending up at Jøstravatnet, where we rub our eyes: for the first time on this trip it's not the sea

reiben uns die Augen: Zum ersten Mal auf dieser Reise haben wir keinen Meeresarm vor uns, sondern einen See. Gefüllt mit Süßwasser aus den Gletschern und Schmelzwasser des Winters zieht er sich in seinem mächtigen Tal dahin. Die Norweger scheint dieses unwirkliche Phänomen so durcheinanderzubringen, dass sie den östlichen See-Arm sogar Kjønesfjord nennen. Ein Fjord, der keiner ist. Am anderen Ende bei Vassenden entwässert der See ganz unauffällig in die Jølstra und dieser kleine Fluss versucht zu retten, was zu retten ist. Knappe 20 Kilometer weit macht er sich als Botschafter des Sees auf die Suche nach dem Meer und hat bei Førde Erfolg: Ab hier mischt sich das Wasser des Jøstravatnet mit dem des Førdefjord und schafft es so in den Nordatlantik.

Wir gehen aber nicht die ganze Reise mit, sondern machen uns bei Holsen in Richtung Osten davon, fliegen über die Berge, und schwingen dann im Slalom hinunter zum Haukedalsvatnet – wieder so ein See, der kein Fjord sein möchte. Und auch der Lauvavatnet, so wie der Viksdalsvatnet ein paar Kilometer weiter, haben keine Lust auf Surf and Turf: Als ernsthafte Seen, ganz ohne Beachlife-Ambitionen, ruhen sie in ihren Tälern. Tiefgrünes Wasser, in das satte Wiesen waten, während sich zu kleinen Wäldern beisammenstehende Nadelbäume vor dem Nasswerden zieren. „Schwarzwald", denken die Schwarzwälder unter uns, „Allgäu" die Allgäuer und „Appalachen" die Pennsylvanier.

Über die turbulente Gaularfjellet-Stiga, ein schwungvolles Serpentinen-Ereignis des Fv13, landen wir aber nach vielen Kilometern erneut am Sognefjord und lassen uns von der Fähre übersetzen. Leise und samtig schwebt das Schiff übers Wasser, wir stehen an der Reling und genießen den Wind, der über die weite Fläche des Fjords streift. Ans Unterwegssein auf dem Fjord haben wir uns längst gewöhnt, wir fahren ganz selbstverständlich an Bord, gehen dann die Schritte vom Parkdeck in die Gänge und Aufenthaltsräume. Farbig gestrichene Treppen, Wasserlachen auf dem stählernen Deck. Der herbe, ölige Duft von Schiffsdiesel streift in Schlieren durch den Wind, mit kräftigem Schub gegen eine glänzend lackierte

we are confronted with, but a lake. Filled with fresh water from the glaciers and snowmelt in winter, it stretches along its mighty valley. The Norwegians seem so confused by this unreal phenomenon that they even call the eastern arm of the lake Kjønesfjord. A fjord by name, but not by nature. At the other end, near Vassenden, the lake drains inconspicuously into the little river Jølstra, which tries to retain what it can of the freshwater character. Acting as an ambassador for the lake, it travels almost 20 kilometers in search of the sea, finally meeting with success at Førde: from here the water from Jøstravatnet mixes with the Førdefjord and thus finally makes it to the North Atlantic.

We're not planning to follow that particular journey, however, but head east at Holsen, speed over the mountains, and then descend on a slalom route to Haukedalsvatnet – another lake that refuses to be a fjord. The same goes for Lakes Lauvavatnet and Viksdalsvatnet a few kilometers further on. There's no feeling of surf and turf here: resting in their valleys, these are serious lakes, with no frivolous beach bum ambitions. The deep green water is enclosed by lush meadows, while little groups of evergreen trees bunch together in small forests, reluctant to get their toes wet. Depending on our nationality, some of us are reminded of Germany's Black Forest or Allgäu regions, while others see echoes of North America's Appalachians. Navigating the turbulent Gaularfjellet-Stiga, a sweeping serpentine on the Fv13 national route, we end up again after many kilometers at the Sognefjord and take the ferry crossing. As the ship sails quietly and sleekly over the water, we stand at the railing and enjoy the wind that sweeps across the wide expanse of the fjord. We have long since become accustomed to this mode of transport on the fjord and drive on board to the manner born, then climbing the steps from the car deck to the corridors and lounges.

Colorfully painted stairs and puddles of water on the steel deck are by now a familiar sight. With the bitter, oily smell of ship's diesel catching in the wind, we push against a varnished wooden door and climb inside the ship – and

VØRINGSFOSSEN

Holztür steigen wir ins Innere des Schiffs – und nun macht sich der Duft eines Fährschiffs in unserer Nase breit: Filterkaffee simmert in großen, glänzenden Maschinen, Hot-Dog-Würstchen räkeln sich in blubbernden Hot Tubs und warten darauf, zwischen weichen Brötchenhälften ihre Bestimmung zu finden. Wir landen auf einem Platz am Fenster oder auf einer Bank im Freien und schauen andächtig zu, wie das manchmal tiefschwarze Wasser des Fjords unter dem Koloss aus Stahl vorüberzieht. Wie an den Ufern Bergkämme wandern, auf und ab tauchen, als seien sie die Rücken von urzeitlichen Riesenwalen.

Am südlichen Ufer des Sognefjord ziehen wir in einem weiten Bogen nach Süden, dann Osten und haben hier Flåm am Ende des Aurlandsfjords erreicht. Vor wenigen Stunden waren wir auf unserer Fahrt über den Aurlandsvegen am Stegastein schon einmal hier, jetzt fahren wir an der Tunneleinfahrt des Lærdaltunnels vorüber in Richtung Hol, stürmen das Serpentinenmonster, mit der die Fv50 nach Südosten das Tal des Sognefjords und seiner Seitenarme verlässt. Fahren in tiefhängenden Wolken über den Berg bis Hagafoss, und dort geht es mit dem Rv7 wieder nach Westen. Wir sind jetzt in den Ausläufern der Hardangervidda angelangt, einer mächtigen Hochebene: Rötliche Farne, Gras und niedriges Buschwerk überziehen das wellige Land, Felsklippen und Steinhügel kauern in der bis zum Horizont reichenden Weite.

Die Straße schnürt gedankenverloren dahin, erst am Vøringfossen wacht sie aus dem Schlummer aus. Hier bricht die Ebene jäh ab, zerbröselt, zerfasert, sackt in tiefe Täler hinunter. Der Rv7 steht im engen Tal vor einem unlösbaren Rätsel – und zieht sich mit eleganten Abwärtskringeln durch Tunnel im Berg aus der Affäre. Und dann hat uns der Hardangerfjord gestellt, ein wahres Ungetüm von Meeresarm, der sich für nahezu 200 Kilometer ins Landesinnere geschoben hat und an seiner tiefsten Stelle

now the smell of ferry life enters our noses: filter coffee simmers in large, shiny machines, hot dogs loll about in bubbling hot pans, waiting to find a home between the two soft halves of a bun. We take a seat by the window or perch on a bench outside and watch intently as the jet-black water of the fjord passes under the colossus of steel. We gaze at the ridges wandering along the banks, diving up and down like the backs of primeval giant whales.

On the southern shore of the Sognefjord we take a widely curving turn south, then east to reach Flåm at the end of the Aurlandsfjord. We were here a few hours ago on our trip following the Aurlandsvegen route at Stegastein, but this time we drive past the entrance to the Lærdal Tunnel in the direction of Hol, storming the series of hairpin bends with which national route Fv50 leaves the valley of the Sognefjord and its side arms to the southeast. We drive over the mountain to Hagafoss in low cloud and from there head west again on the Rv7. We are now in the foothills of the Hardangervidda, a mighty plateau: reddish ferns, grass and low scrub cover the rolling landscape, crags and cairns crouch in the expanse as far as the eye can see. The road is lost in thought, waking up from its slumber only at Vøringfossen. Here the plains break off abruptly, crumbling, fraying, plunging into deep valleys.

The Rv7 faces an impossible puzzle in the narrow valley, restoring order with an elegant downward twist through tunnels in the mountain. And then we encounter the Hardangerfjord, a genuine behemoth that has pushed its way inland for almost 200 kilometers, over 800 meters deep at its deepest point. When we move on to the Sørfjord at Kinsarvik, these gargantuan dimensions are no longer obvious. The landscape seems friendly and welcoming, fruit grows on the slopes, scattered houses look out over the narrow fjord. You could easily imagine yourself on a lake in Switzerland.

Fahren in tiefhängenden Wolken über den Berg bis Hagafoss, und dort geht es mit dem Rv7 wieder nach Westen. Wir sind jetzt in den Ausläufern der Hardangervidda angelangt, einer mächtigen Hochebene: Rötliche Farne, Gras und niedriges Buschwerk überziehen das wellige Land, Felsklippen und Steinhügel kauern in der bis zum Horizont reichenden Weite.

We drive over the mountain to Hagafoss in low cloud and from there head west again on the Rv7. We are now in the foothills of the Hardangervidda, a mighty plateau: reddish ferns, grass and low scrub cover the rolling landscape, crags and cairns crouch in the expanse as far as the eye can see.

über 800 Meter tief ist. Als wir bei Kinsarvik in den Seitenarm Sørfjord wechseln, sind diese monströsen Ausmaße aber keineswegs offensichtlich. Die Landschaft wirkt lieblich und freundlich, in den Hanglagen wächst Obst, verstreute Häuser schauen über den schmalen Fjord – das hier könnte ohne allzu viel Fantasie auch irgendwie an einem See in der Schweiz sein. Dass gleich um die Ecke mit Wasser gefüllte Abgründe gähnen, sieht man dieser Landschaft nicht an. Vierzig Kilometer weit folgen wir dem Fjord, ziehen immer weiter im Tal nach Süden, auch wenn das Wasser des Fjords längst zurückgeblieben ist. Bei Skare geht es hinauf in felsige Höhen, wieder schneidet ein Tunnel schnurgerade durchs Gebirge, und nun sind wir bei Horda angelangt.

Wir wenden nach Südwesten, bleiben hartnäckig am Gas und als wir nach vielen Kilometern am Erfjord angekommen sind, haben wir das Inland eindeutig zurückgelassen. Die Routenführung wechselt wieder in den beinahe schon vergessenen Kampf mit der Schärenküste: Inselhopping, Bergumrundungen, Fährpassagen, Tunnel-Kilometer. Als Krönung wartet dann der Ryfylke-Tunnel auf uns, der sich nahezu 300 Meter tief und viele Kilometer weit in die Erdkruste wühlt, um unter dem Hørgefjord nach Stavanger zu gelangen. Das hört sich spektakulär an – ist am Ende aber eben einfach eine Röhre. Deckenleuchten, die in stetem Rhythmus nach hinten fliegen, Lüftungs-Rotoren, Zwielicht – den Nervenkitzel und die Gänsehaut-Effekte dieser Ingenieurs-Großtat muss man sich schon vorstellen.

Looking at this landscape, you'd never guess the water-filled abysses just around the corner.

We follow the fjord for forty kilometers, moving further and further south into the valley, leaving the water of the fjord far behind us. At Skare, the road takes us to rocky heights and another tunnel cuts straight through the mountains. Arriving at Horda, we turn southwest, still stepping hard on the gas. When we make it to the Erfjord after many kilometers, we have clearly left the Norwegian interior behind. The route reverts to the almost forgotten struggle with the skerry coast: island hopping, mountain tours, ferry passages, kilometers of tunnels.

The crowning glory is the Ryfylke Tunnel, which probes almost 300 meters deep and many kilometers into the earth's crust to reach Stavanger under the Hørgefjord. Although that sounds spectacular – in the end it's just another tube. Overhead lights fly past in a constant rhythm in the twilight, interrupted only by ventilation fans. You have to imagine the thrills and goosebumps of this feat of engineering for yourself.

HOTEL

EILERT SMITH HOTEL
NORDBOGATA 8
4006 STAVANGER
WWW.EILERTSMITH.NO

BORETUNET
BORESTRANDA
4352 KLEPP
WWW.BORETUNET.NO

RØLDALSFJELLET

ROAD 520 HARA · SAUDA

ROAD 520 HARA - SAUDA

LÆRDAL STAVANGER

Rund um die zwei großen Fjorde des norwegischen Westens bewegen wir uns auf der vierten Etappe – die Reise beginnt am Sognefjord. Auf einem weiten Bogen nach Norden dringen wir bis zu den Ausläufern des Jostedals-breen vor: Die mächtige Gletscherhaube bedeckt nach wie vor große Gebiete im Landesinneren, allerdings trägt auch hier der Klimawandel stark zu einem deutlichen Abschmelzen des Eises bei. Entlang des großen Jølstra-vatnet-Sees rollen wir nun nach Westen, vollenden dann unsere Runde zurück zum Sognefjord. Über den Vika-fjelsvegen und dann die E 16 nach Osten landen wir bei Flåm und damit beinahe wieder am Ausgangspunkt. Von hier aus ziehen wir aber an Steine vorüber weiter ins Landesinnere zurück, fahren in die Region Viken und schlagen erst bei Hagafoss erneut einen Haken. Nun geht es über die Seeenlandschaft südlich des Haugastøl, die nördlichen Ausläufer der Hardangervidda-Hochebene und die tiefen Taleinschnitte in der Region rund um den Vøringfossen zum zweiten Fjord-Riesen der norwegischen Westküste: dem Hardangerfjord. Entlang seines Sørf-jord-Ausläufers zielen wir nun geradewegs nach Süden, bis wir in der von Halbinseln und Inseln geprägten Küs-tenlandschaft rund um Stavanger angekommen sind. Hier, in der viertgrößten Stadt Norwegens, haben wir den Ausgangspunkt zur letzten Etappe erreicht.

—

On the fourth stage of our trip, we circumnavigate the two large fjords of western Norway – the journey begins at the Sognefjord. Moving in a wide northerly arc, we advance to the foothills of the Jostedalsbreen glacier: the mighty glacial cap still covers large inland areas, but climate change is also making a significant contribution to significant melting of the ice here. We now travel west along the expanse of Jølstravatnet Lake, completing our trip by looping back to the Sognefjord. Following the Vikafjelsvegen route and then the E 16 to the east we end up at Flåm and thus almost back at our starting point. From here, however, we turn back further inland across stones, traveling into the Viken region only to make another detour at Hagafoss. We now cross the lake-filled landscape south of the Haugastøl, the northern foothills of the Hardangervidda plateau and the deep valleys in the region around the Vøringfossen to reach the second gigantic fjord of the Norwegian west coast: the Hardangerfjord. We now head straight south along Sørfjord, the main fjord's little sister, until we arrive in the coastal landscape around Stavanger, characterized by numerous peninsulas and islands. Here, in Norway's fourth largest city, we have reached the starting point for the last stage of our trip.

890 KM • 2-3 TAGE // 553 MILES • 2-3 DAYS

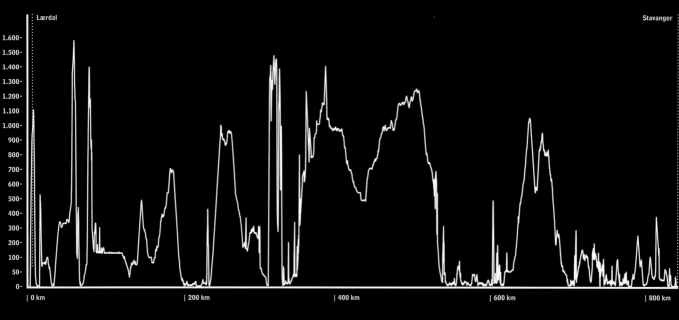

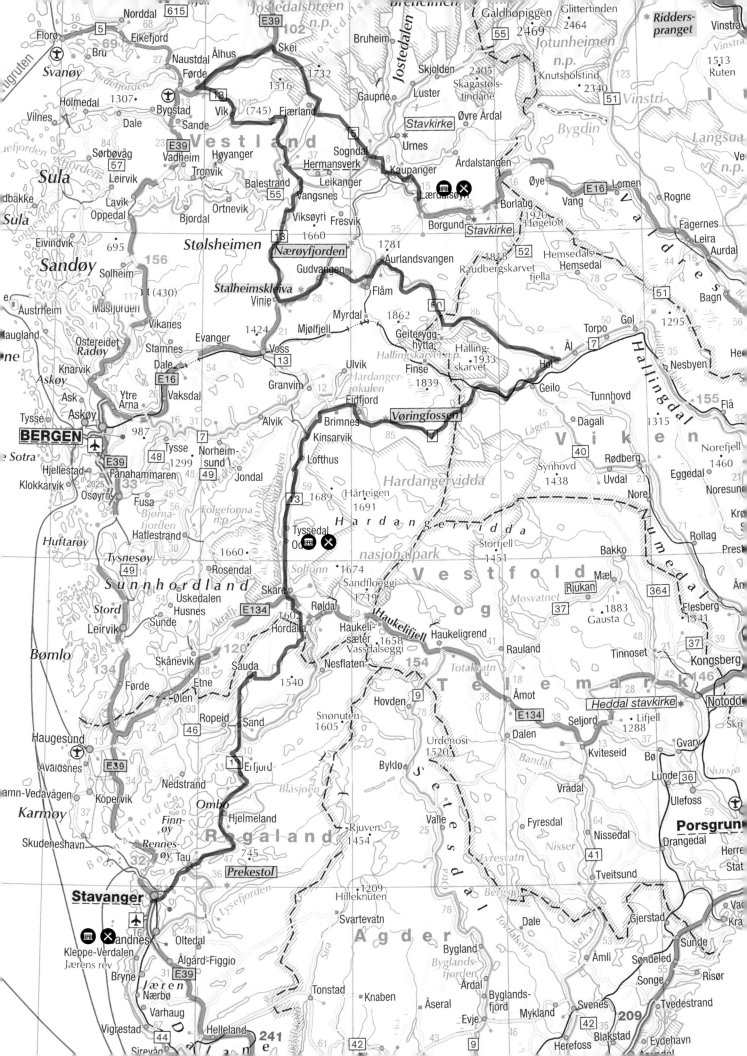

STAVANGER KRISTIANSAND

400 KM • 1-2 TAGE // 249 MILES • 1-2 DAYS

Guten Morgen, Stavanger. Deine Sommernacht war voller Wunder. Selbst hier unten im Süden Norwegens bleibt die Sonne zu dieser Jahreszeit noch lange wach, lässt gut gelaunte Menschen bis in den Morgen hinein durch die Gassen ziehen. Übers Kopfsteinpflaster der Fargegaten mit ihren bunten Hausfassaden, ein Blumenstrauß aus Farbe. Lila und Orange, Blau und Gelb, Rot und Grün und Rosarot.

—

Good morning, Stavanger. You treated us to a summer's night full of wonders. It remains bright long into the night at this time of year, even down here in southern Norway, giving good-humored people an opportunity to roam the streets well into the morning hours. We cross the cobblestones of the Fargegaten with its colorful facades like a bouquet of flowers, purple and orange, blue and yellow, red and green and pink.

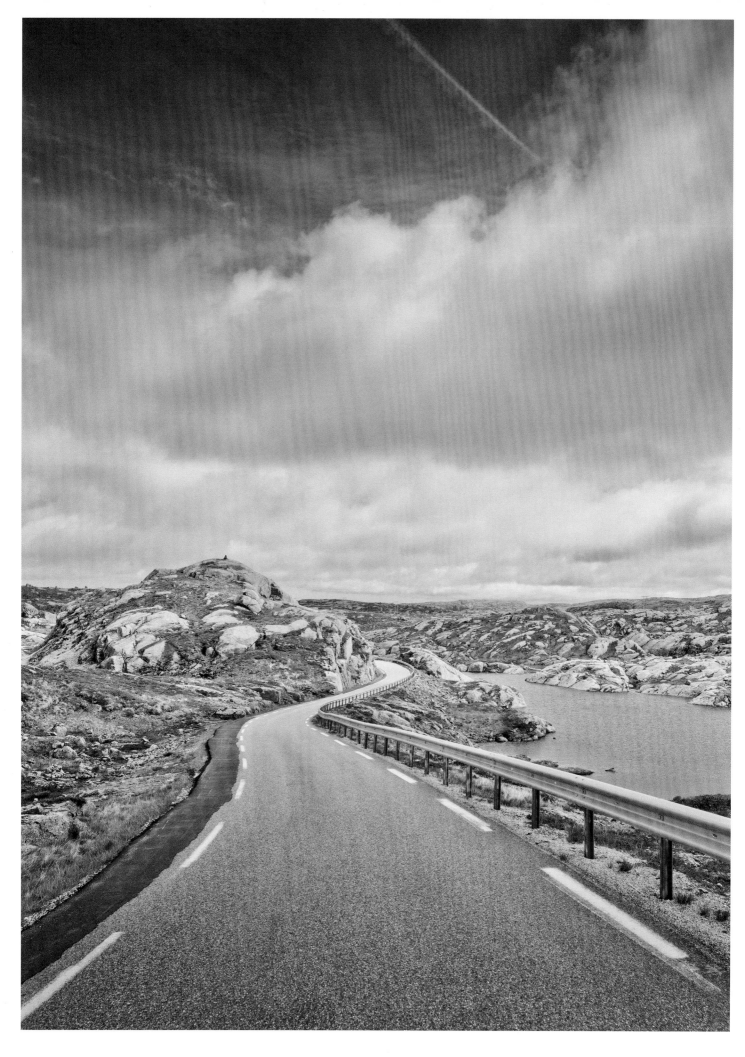

Aber auch sonst ist die Innenstadt gefüllt mit Licht und Farbe und Lachen, die Restaurants gehen bis hinaus auf die Terrassen und Straßen. Und wenn dann die Nacht hereinbricht, ist sie nicht düster und schwarz, sondern eine dunkelblaue Dämmerung voller Schimmer und Glanz. Aus den Häusern dringt oranger Schein, Kirchtürme und Fassaden werden beleuchtet, am Himmel gleiten aquarellgraue Wolken über einen fahlgelben Hintergrund. Und wenn man dann endlich ins Bett fällt, ist da draußen immer noch der Widerschein der Sonnenstrahlen, die verstohlen als Letzte um die Häuser ziehen. So schüchtern sind sie aber nicht allzu lange, schon früh am Morgen scheint die Sonne wieder hell und kräftig, lässt die Schläfer ihre Augen reiben. Es ist Sommer in Skandinavien, schlafen kann man im Winter.

Also raus aus der Stadt – aber vorher eine Wahl treffen: Soll es direkt nach Süden gehen, mit dem Frafjord in Richtung unseres letzten Etappenziels an der Skagerrak-Küste, oder darf es ein Abstecher zum ganz sicher hollywoodreifen Preikestolen sein, dem entsetzlichen Felsen über dem Lysefjord? – Bis Høle haben Unschlüssige noch Zeit für die Entscheidung, hier könnte man an der Fähre von Lauvvik nach Oanes noch den Abstecher zum Lysefjord machen. Der verlässt hier den Høgsfjord nach Nordosten, legt hinter der Lysefjord-Brücke so richtig los: Majestätisch, traumhaft, bedrohlich. Von hinten schleicht man sich an, biegt am Botnefjord auf den Preikestolvegen ab und darf dann das Auto am Parkplatz zurücklassen. Jetzt geht es nur noch zu Fuß voran, über Felsen und struppigen, offenen Wald, immer höher hinauf. Und dann landet der viel begangene Fußweg an der leuchtend hellen Granitklippe über dem Lysefjord. Auf den letzten Metern ahnt man, dass es hier tief ins Tal hinab geht, aber erst am Rand der Preikestolen-Klippe ist klar, wie tief: schwindelerregend, magnetisch anziehend, 600 Meter freier Fall. Vier Stunden sollte man für dieses schweißtreibende Erlebnis mindestens einplanen. Wer seine Akrophobie auf der Kanzel des „Predigtstuhls" länger kultivieren mag, braucht auch noch mehr.

Zurück in Høle geht es dann endgültig auf die letzten Abschnitte unserer Reise, rund 350 Kilometer liegen vor uns auf dem Weg nach Kristiansand. Über die 508 schwingen wir nach Süden, bis zum Oltedal-See, und dort steigt die Straße hinunter zum Høgsfjord. Die wenigen Meter am

However the city center is also filled with light, color and laughter from a different source, as restaurants spill onto the terraces and streets. When night finally falls, the sky is not somber and black, but rather a shimmering, dark blue twilight. An orange glow emanates from the houses. The church towers and facades are illuminated and clouds of watercolor gray glide against a pale yellow background. As you finally fall into bed, the last reflections of the sun's rays drop behind the houses. They don't stay away for too long and early in the morning the sun is bright and strong again, making the sleepers rub their eyes. It's summertime in Scandinavia and there'll be plenty of time to sleep in winter.

So let's get ourselves out of town – but first a choice needs to be made: do you want to head straight south, following the Frafjord towards our last stop on the Skagerrak coast, or would you prefer to take a detour to the Preikestolen, the terrifying rock that towers over the Lysefjord like something from a Hollywood horror movie? – If you're unsure, you still have time to make a final decision before you reach Høle, where you could still make a detour to the Lysefjord on the ferry from Lauvvik to Oanes. The geological formation stretches away from the Høgsfjord to the north-east and really gets into its stride beyond the Lysefjord Bridge: majestic, dreamlike, menacing. You sneak up on it from behind, turning onto Preikestolvegen at the Botnefjord and then leaving your car in the parking lot. The only way forward at this point is on foot, crossing rocks and scrubby, open forest, climbing higher and higher. Finally, the well-trodden path ends up at the bright granite cliff above the Lysefjord. As you complete the last few meters you get the feeling that you are close to a steep precipice high above the valley, but it is only at the edge of the Preikestolen cliff that you realize how deep the drop in fact is: dizzying, magnetically attractive – a 600-meter free fall. You should plan at least four hours for this strenuous experience. If you want to test your acrophobia for even longer on the "pulpit", you'll need a bit more time.

Back in Høle we finally start the last sections of our journey. Around 350 kilometers lie ahead of us on the way to Kristiansand. We swing south via Route 508, to Lake Oltedal, and there the road descends to the Høgsfjord. The few meters of the route that stick close to the shore give us

Ufer entlang reichen aber nur für einen kurzen Blick hinaus aufs Wasser und dann sind wir auch wieder unterwegs ins Landesinnere: über die 450 entlang der Dirdalsåna nach Osten. Am Ende des Tals zwängt sich der Fluss zusammen mit der Straße durch einen engen Durchlass, zieht in die Berge hinauf, ins Byrkedal. Zwischen den Kämmen derber Felsriffe geht es immer weiter, durch ein Land, in dem Trolle mit Felsen Murmeln spielen, Schafe dem Auto neugierig hinterherschauen und sich selbst im Sommer noch Schneeflecken im Schatten halten. Oben im Sirdal haben wir dann wieder eine Abzweigung erreicht – die Straße zum östlichen Ende des Lysefjords. Der hat nördlich von uns sein Ende bei Lysebotn erreicht und hierhin geht es: 45 Kilometer über wilde Serpentinen, über ein elegant ins Land gefrästes Asphaltband, das schmal und schlingernd Meter macht. Kraut und Birken, Unterholz und Flechten säumen den Weg. Die Felsen am Rand der Straße sind bunt und gescheckt, Grau, Ocker, Rot, sie glänzen vom Wasser, das aus ihnen sickert. Der Erdboden verwandelt sich in eine derbe Gebirgslandschaft, voller Hügel, Berge und Schluchten. Seen sammeln sich, Flüsse und Bäche streifen durchs Land. Irgendwann ist da nur noch mit Flechten überzogener Granit und karges Gras, das in den Ritzen Halt gefunden hat – und dann stürzt sich die Straße hinunter zum Lysefjord. Es kommt uns wie eine Ewigkeit vor, als wir an seinem anderen Ende, hoch oben über seinem Spiegel auf dem Preikestolen waren.

Zurück in Sinnes fahren wir über die 468 geradewegs nach Süden, wechseln in Tonstad auf die 42 und jetzt sind wir am Ufer des Sirdalsvatnet unterwegs. 28 Kilometer lang und bis zu 370 Meter tief zieht sich der schmale See in einer Art Rinne dahin und wieder verschwimmen die Kategorien: Ist es ein Fjord? Ein Fluss? Wirklich ein See? – Die Straße hält Abstand zum Ufer, schnürt auf einem Sockel über der Wasseroberfläche dahin, immer weiter. Wir sind längst wieder in jenen stoischen Trab verfallen, der das Fahren in Norwegen so oft ausmacht: Hartnäckiges Meilenfressen, ohne Eile, Stunde um Stunde. Und dann zwingt uns die Topografie weg vom See, der mit seinem steil abfallenden Ufer endlich in Ruhe gelassen werden will. Die Straße drängt sich immer weiter

just enough time for a brief gaze at the water and then we are on our way inland again, on Route 450 along the Dirdalsåna river to the east. At the end of the valley, the river and road squeeze themselves through a narrow gorge and head up into the mountains, into Byrkedal. Between the crests of rough rocky reefs, our journey continues through a landscape where you could imagine trolls playing marbles with boulders. Sheep watch the car in mild curiosity and patches of snow remain on shaded ground even in summer. At the top of Sirdal we reach another junction – the road to the eastern end of the Lysefjord. It reached its end north of us at Lysebotn, where we are headed: 45 kilometers over wild switchbacks, over an asphalt strip that has been elegantly incised into the countryside in a narrow, snaking ribbon. Wild plants and birches, undergrowth and lichen line the way. The rocks at the edge of the road are multicolored and mottled, glistening gray, ocher and red as water seeps out of them. The ground turns into a rough mountain landscape, full of hills, mountains and gorges. Lakes form, rivers and streams criss-cross the country. At some point all that is left is lichen-covered granite and sparse grass that has found a hold in the cracks – and then the road plunges down to the Lysefjord. It feels like an eternity until we reach the other end, high above the level of the Preikestolen.

Back in Sinnes we head straight south on Route 468, change to Route 42 in Tonstad and find ourselves on the shores of Lake Sirdalsvatnet. The narrow lake is 28 kilometers long and up to 370 meters deep, forming a kind of channel and causing the categories to become blurred again: Is it a fjord? Or maybe a river? A lake? Really? – The road maintains its distance from the shore, clinging to a ledge above the water's surface, traveling ever onward. We've long since fallen into that stoic pattern that so often characterizes driving in Norway, crunching the miles, hour after hour in a persistent unhurried manner. The topography then forces us away from the lake, its steep and precipitous shores signaling it wants to be left alone. The road presses ever further east, then changes its rhythm again, switching from stately straights to winding bends within just a few kilometers.

HOTEL

THE BOLDER SKYLODGE
4110 FORSAND
WWW.THEBOLDER.NO

HOTEL & RESTAURANT

HOTEL Q42
TOLLBODGATA 70
4608 KRISTIANSAND
WWW.KRISTIANSANDKONGRESSENTER.
NO/Q42-HOTEL

BONDER I BYEN
RÅDHUSGATA 16
4611 KRISTIANSAND
WWW.BONDERIBYEN.COM

BOEN FARM
DONNESTADVEIEN 341
4658 TVEIT
WWW.BOENGAARD.NO

nach Osten, dann verändert sie erneut ihren Rhythmus: von gemächlich-geradeaus auf schwungvoll-kurvend innerhalb weniger Kilometer. In Buchten am Ufer von kleinen Seen haben sich Gehöfte und Weiler niedergelassen, Holzhäuser in Rot und Weiß halten vorsichtigen Abstand zueinander – Platz genug ist hier ja. Lupinen stehen am Ufer grüner Bäche stramm, Wasserlinsen bilden Teppiche auf Teichen. Gruppen von Birken winken mit tanzenden, wirbelnden Blättern in einen blassblauen Himmel. Einfache Holzkirchen halten Wache auf Friedhöfen, in denen schroff zugehauene Grabsteine lose Spaliere bilden und sauber gemähter Rasen für Ordnung sorgt. Für Mitteleuropäer wirkt das Land immer noch einsam und leer, aber die Bevölkerungsdichte nimmt zu. Unmerklich zuerst, dann immer mehr. Angekommen im Tal der Songdalselva ist die Welt dann unbestreitbar domestiziert: Wohngebiete ziehen sich entlang der Straße, Industriebetriebe klotzen schmucklos auf ihren Parzellen und die Straße ist breit geworden. Benötigt Kreisverkehre und Ampeln, um den Verkehr zu kontrollieren, landet dann zusammen mit der Songsdalelva bei Høllen am Meer. Und das ist nicht der Nordatlantik, mit dem wir es bisher im Westen zu tun hatten, sondern die von kleinen Inseln gesprenkelte Küste des Skagerrak. Die Nordsee zwischen Norwegens Südküste und Dänemark. Bootsanleger krallen sich auf Felsen in den Buchten, Häuser schauen aufs Wasser hinaus, daneben strebt die Straße ruhig nach Osten, in Richtung Kristiansand.

Die große Stadt im Süden umklammert die Mündung des Kristiansandfjords, macht sich zwischen Hügeln und dem Meer breit. Brücken überspannen die Meeresarme in der Stadt, Kirchen, Hochhäuser und Wohnblocks ragen aus dem dicht gepackten Häusermeer empor. Vor allem der Hafen nimmt viel Raum ein, seinetwegen sind die Menschen hierher gekommen. Auch wir. Unsere Fähre wartet bereits: ein mächtiger Koloss, fest vertäut am Kai, die Ladeluke weit geöffnet. Es dauert nur wenige Sekunden, über die Laderampe in den Bauch des Schiffs zu fahren – hinaus aus Norwegen. Zwischen drei und vier Stunden dauert dann die Fahrt über die Nordsee, hinüber nach Hirtshals in Dänemark. Genügend Zeit, um nicht nur einen, sondern gleich zwei Hotdogs zu essen.

Farmsteads and hamlets have settled in the bays on the shores of little lakes, groups of red and white houses keep a careful distance from one another – after all there's plenty of space here. Serried ranks of lupines stand to attention on the banks of green streams, carpets of duckweed form on ponds. Clusters of birch trees wave their dancing, swirling leaves in a pale blue sky. Simple wooden churches keep vigil over cemeteries where roughly hewn tombstones form loose rows and neatly mown lawns maintain order.

To Central European eyes the countryside still seems isolated and empty, however signs of civilization begin to increase, barely noticeable at first, then more and more. Arriving in the valley of the Songdalselva River, our surroundings are undeniably more domesticated: residential areas stretch along the road, industrial enterprises sit squarely on their sites and the road has become wider, needing roundabouts and traffic lights to control the traffic, then ending up together with the Songsdalelva at the sea at Høllen. Instead of the North Atlantic that we've been dealing with in the West, this is the island-dotted coast of the Skagerrak, the North Sea between Norway's southern coast and Denmark. Piers cling to the rocks in the bays, houses look out over the water, and next to them the road quietly heads east towards Kristiansand.

The major city of the south hugs the mouth of the Kristiansandfjord, spreading out between hills and sea. Bridges span the arms of the sea within the city. Churches, high-rise buildings and blocks of flats tower above a densely packed sea of houses. The port in particular takes up a lot of space, providing one of the main reasons why people come here. That includes us. Our ferry is already waiting: a mighty colossus, firmly moored by the quay, its hatch gaping open. It only takes a few seconds to drive down the loading dock into the hold of the ship – out of Norway. The trip across the North Sea to Hirtshals in Denmark takes between three and four hours. Enough time to eat not one, but two hot dogs.

LYSEBOTN

STAVANGER KRISTIANSAND

Ungefähr auf Höhe von Stavanger endet die von Fjorden zerklüftete Westküste Norwegens. Die Stadt liegt am nördlichsten Punkt eines weiten Bogens, den die Küste von hier aus nach Osten schlägt und dann bei Kristiansand in Richtung Oslo verläuft. Unsere letzte Etappe führt über diese Südspitze Norwegens, mit einem letzten, kurvenreichen Abstecher zum Ende des Lysefjords sagen wir der Welt dieser atemberaubend schönen Meeresarme auf Wiedersehen. Übrigens: Am westlichen Ende des Lysefjord, wenige Kilometer nach seinem Beginn im Høgsfjord, liegt einer der spektakulärsten Orte Norwegens: Der 600 Meter tief zum Fjord hin frei abfallende Preikestolen (Predigtstuhl) war schon in einigen Hollywood-Filmen landschaftlicher Hauptdarsteller. Er ist nur zu Fuß zu erreichen, je nach Jahreszeit ist man zum Leidwesen von Landschaftsschützern hier auch nicht ganz allein unterwegs. Wer also den Preikestolen besuchen möchte, sollte das möglichst nicht im Sommer tun, sondern rücksichtsvoll und an einem ruhigeren Tag des Jahres. Die weitere Route zum langgezogenen Sirdalsvatnet-See, dann quer über die Berge zum Lygne-See und schließlich nach Süden, an die Küste bei Kristiansand, verläuft dagegen deutlich ruhiger. Ein letztes Mal sind wir im wilden Inland Norwegens unterwegs, dann haben wir das Ziel am Skagerrak erreicht.

—

Norway's west coast, which is studded with fjords, ends roughly at the level of Stavanger. The city lies at the northernmost point of a wide arc as the coast sweeps east from here and then towards Oslo at Kristiansand. The last leg of our trip takes us across this southern tip of Norway, with a final, winding detour to the end of the Lysefjord, where we say goodbye to the world of breathtakingly beautiful inlets. By the way: the western end of the Lysefjord, a few kilometers after its beginning in the Høgsfjord, is one of the most spectacular places in Norway: the 600-meter-deep Preikestolen (pulpit), which drops straight down to the fjord, has provided the backdrop for a number of Hollywood movies. It can only be reached on foot. Depending on the season, it can get quite busy here, much to the chagrin of the conservationists. So, if you want to visit the Preikestolen, you should try to avoid doing so in summer, choosing instead a quieter time of year. The route continues to the elongated expanse of Sirdalsvatnet Lake, then crosses the mountains to Lake Lygne and finally heads south to the coast at Kristiansand and is much quieter. One last time we take a route that passes through the wild interior of Norway, before reaching our destination at the Skagerrak.

400 KM • 1-2 TAGE // 249 MILES • 1-2 DAYS

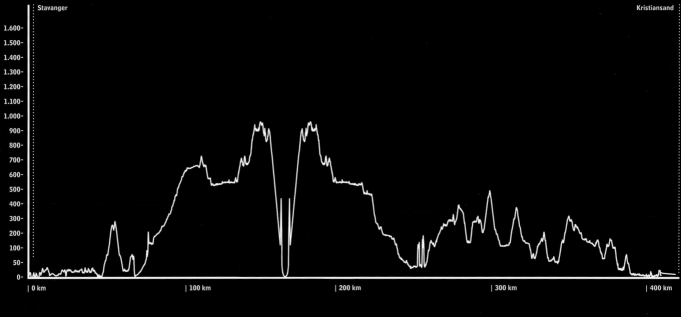

JOHANNES EINEMO & THE LAERDAL SØRENRING

Und dann wäre da noch der Laerdalsørenring. Kenner der internationalen Rennstrecken-Szene dürften bei seiner Erwähnung ratlos mit den Achseln zucken, dabei hat es diese Strecke wirklich in sich. Entstanden aus trockenem skandinavischem Humor und völlig durchgebrannter Auto-Leidenschaft handelt es sich nicht um eine „Rennstrecke" im eigentlichen Sinne, der „Laerdalsørenring" ist vielmehr eine Huldigung des legendären Nürburgrings in einer Übertragung auf die Bergstraßen rund um den Laerdals-Fjord. Also: kein Fahren im Renntempo, sondern im herunterskalierten Groove öffentlicher Passstraßen. Versunken im Rhythmus der Kurven, verloren im Flow – aber sicher und legal diesseits des Grenzbereichs.

Erfunden hat diese im Kern geniale Skurrilität Johannes Einemo vom Laerdalsørenhotels (www.lardalsorenhotel.no), der mit seinem Team einerseits rustikal-charmante Gastfreundschaft in den Räumen eines herrlichen Holzgebäudes in Laerdalsøri pflegt, andererseits modernen Fahrmaschinen ganz und gar nicht abgeneigt ist: Nach einer Nacht in vollendet nostalgischer Atmosphäre den Porsche 911 oder die KTM Super Duke mieten und dann in die Berge brennen – das geht hier. Und natürlich darf man auch sein eigenes Material ausführen, die Straßen der Gegend ziehen Automobilclubs und fahrende Gesellen regelrecht magisch an. Fehlt also nur noch eine Insider-Sicht, die dem Gast aus der Ferne eine Abkürzung zu den besten Erlebnissen und Strecken zeigt ... An dieser Stelle kommt der von der Atmosphäre der Nürburgring-Nordschleife inspirierte Laerdalsørenring ins Spiel – eine klug und mit mächtigem Kurven-Know-how kuratierte Abfolge von vier Strecken in der Umgebung. Fahren an Fjorden und in den Bergen, über Pässe und Gletscher, auf Asphalt, Schotter und sogar im Schnee.

We shouldn't forget to mention the Laerdalsørenring. Although connoisseurs of the international race track scene might shrug their shoulders in ignorance on hearing this name, this track really does have it all. Born out of a dry Scandinavian sense of humor and a total runaway passion for cars, the "Laerdalsørenring" isn't really a "race track" in the true sense, but rather a name coined in homage to the legendary Nürburgring and applied to the mountain roads around the Laerdalsfjord. In other words, you can't go driving at racing speaed, but instead have to content yourself with the downscaled groove of public mountain passes – lost in the rhythm of the curves, lost in the flow – but safe and within the legal limit.

Basically a scurrilously ingenious joke, the name was the brainchild of Johannes Einemo of the Laerdalsøren Hotel (www.lardalsorenhotel.no), who, along with his team, is pleased to offer charming rustic hospitality in a magnificent wooden building in Laerdal. In addition, Einemo's team also has a special affinity with modern automobiles: after spending a night in a completely nostalgic setting, guests can rent a Porsche 911 or KTM Super Duke and burn a trail into the mountains. Of course, people are also welcome to drive their own cars and the area's roads attract automobile clubs and other petrol heads as if by magic. All that's missing is a source of insider tips to guide guests to the best experiences and tracks. This is where the Laerdalsørenring, inspired by the atmosphere of the Nürburgring-Nordschleife, comes into play – a clever sequence of four routes around the area, expertly curated to include thrilling bends and taking in fjords and mountains, passes and glaciers, tarmac, gravel and even snow.

ASK THE LOCAL

Aksel Lund Svindal strahlt einfach positive Energie aus – der norwegische Skirennläufer gehört zu den Besten seines Fachs, ist unter anderem zweimaliger Olympiasieger und fünffacher Weltmeister und hat auch sonst alles gewonnen, was es zu gewinnen gibt. Auch die Widrigkeiten des Lebens werfen ihn nicht aus der Bahn, was er in seiner Karriere mehrfach bewiesen hat. Nach heftigen Unfällen kehrte er stets umso motivierter zurück. Nebenbei ist er ein richtig sympathischer Typ, erfolgreicher Unternehmer und auch Markenbotschafter bei Porsche. Und das nicht von ungefähr: Aksel Svindal ist nicht nur auf zwei Skiern ein Ass, sondern auch hinter dem Steuer seines Cayman GT4 bei der Porsche Sprint Challenge Scandinavia. Positive Energie eben.

–

Aksel Lund Svindal simply radiates positive energy – the Norwegian ski racer is one of the best in his field, including two Olympic champion and five world champion titles, and has also won everything else there is to win. Even the adversities of life do not throw him off course, as he has proven several times in his career. After serious accidents, he has always come back with even greater determination. In addition, he is a really likeable guy, a successful entrepreneur and also a brand ambassador for Porsche. And that's no coincidence: Aksel Svindal is not only an ace on two skis, but also behind the wheel of his Cayman GT4 in the Porsche Sprint Challenge Scandinavia. Positive energy, after all.

Was macht Aksel Svindal, wenn er nicht in seinem Porsche oder auf Skiern unterwegs ist? Manchmal muss ich in einem Büro sitzen und arbeiten. Wenn das nicht der Fall ist, bin ich gern draußen und treibe Sport. Und im Sommer nicht auf Skiern, sondern auf Rädern oder auf dem Wasser: Radfahren oder Wingfoiling.

Skifahren und Autofahren – gibt es da Gemeinsamkeiten? Beides ist sehr dynamisch, und bei beidem geht es um Kurven und Schwünge. Es macht keinen Spaß, nur geradeaus zu fahren.

Wo ist mehr Adrenalin im Spiel – beim Fahren oder beim Skifahren? Skifahren auf hohem Niveau ist sicherlich der größte Adrenalinstoß, den ich je erlebt habe. Aber auf der Rennstrecke gibt es das auch. Besonders, wenn man im Rennen von Autos umgeben ist.

Welche Autos fährst du im Moment? Welches würdest du gerne mal fahren? Und welches Auto findest du einfach nur hoffnungslos gut? Ich fahre den Taycan Cross Turismo als Alltagsauto. Das ist ein perfektes Auto, das alles kann. Ich liebe ihn. Auf der Rennstrecke fahre ich einen Cayman GT4 Rennwagen. Ich frage mich, ob ein GT4 RS nicht das perfekte Straßenauto für Norwegen wäre.

Sportwagenfahren in Norwegen ist nicht gerade eine ideale Kombination. Oder etwa doch? Wenn Sie Kurven und schöne Aussichten mögen, ist Norwegen der perfekte Ort dafür. Wenn Sie schnell fahren wollen, sollten Sie auf der deutschen Autobahn bleiben :)

Wenn Norwegen-Besucher nur eine Strecke fahren dürften, wo würdest du sie hinschicken? Oh, schwierige Frage. Ich würde empfehlen, von Tromsø nach Trondheim zu fahren. Und ein paar Umwege zu machen. Das ist eine lange Fahrt, aber sie ist wunderschön. Man kann sogar die Lofoten meiden (um dem Touristenstrom zu entgehen), und es ist immer noch absolut beeindruckend.

What does Aksel Svindal do when he's not skiing or driving his Porsche? Sometimes I need to spend time working in the office. When that's not the case, I like to be outside and do sports. And in the summer that is not on skis, it's on wheels or on water. Cycling or wingfoiling.

Skiing and driving – do they have anything in common? Both are very dynamic and both are about turns and curves. It's no fun to go in a straight line.

Which involves more adrenaline – driving or skiing? Skiing at a high level is undoubtedly the biggest adrenaline rush I've ever had. But being on the racetrack does bring out some of the same feelings. Especially in a race when you are surrounded by cars.

What cars are you driving right now? Which one would you like to drive? And which car do you just find ridiculously good? I drive the Taycan Cross Turismo as my everyday car. It's a perfect do-it-all car. I love it. On the track, I drive a Cayman GT4 race car. I wonder whether a GT4 RS would be the perfect roadcar for Norway.

Driving sports cars in Norway is not exactly a perfect fit. Or is it? If you like curves and beautiful views, it's the perfect place to go. If you want to go fast you should stay on the German Autobahn. :)

If visitors to Norway were only allowed to drive one route, where would you send them? That's a tough one. I would recommend going from Tromsø to Trondheim. And to take some detours along the way. It's a long drive but it's so beautiful. You can even bypass the Lofoten Islands (to avoid the tourist traffic), and it's still absolutely amazing.

What are your favorite routes outside of Norway? There are some beautiful mountain passes in the Alps. Especially in Italy and Switzerland. Like the roads from

Was sind Deine Lieblingsstrecken außerhalb von Norwegen? Es gibt einige wunderschöne Bergpässe in den Alpen. Vor allem in Italien und der Schweiz. Zum Beispiel die Straßen von Cortina durch die Dolomiten. Über das Stilfser Joch und weiter in die Schweiz.

Was ist für Dich „Norwegen-Feeling" und warum sollte jeder einmal in Norwegen gewesen sein? Die Fjorde und die Berge, die sie umgeben. Und dann ein Zwischenstopp und Erdbeeren aus der Region probieren. Man sollte hinfahren, denn Fotos werden dem Land nicht gerecht. Nicht einmal die im CURVES Magazin.

Haben die Norweger eine andere Einstellung zum Autofahren als die Menschen in anderen Ländern? Hmmm. Gute Frage. Sie sind vorsichtiger als Südeuropäer, denke ich. Aber sie sind besser im Kurvenfahren als der Durchschnittsfahrer aus Deutschland, Dänemark usw. Und wir fahren viele Elektroautos.

Lassen wir das Auto mal beiseite: Wo ist für Sie der schönste Ort in Norwegen? Es gibt viele Orte auf der von mir beschriebenen Strecke: Tromsø bis Trondheim. Die Insel Senja ist einer von ihnen.

Elektroantrieb oder Verbrennungsmotor? Ich bin ein großer Fan des Elektroantriebs für den täglichen Gebrauch. Und ich glaube, wir werden bald einige ziemlich coole elektrische Rennwagen sehen. Für beides müssen wir eine funktionierende Infrastruktur schaffen. Die Leistung der Autos ist bereits großartig.

Mit einem Beifahrer oder allein? Allein, ha ha. Klingt seltsam, aber ich genieße die Ruhe und den freien Kopf.

Und was läuft im Radio? Ein Podcast für die langen Fahrten mit weiten Entfernungen. Ein paar Rockklassiker für die Spritztour. Aber auch einfach nur Ruhe. Radio aus. Das Auto und die Natur genießen.

Cortina through the Dolomites. Up the Stelvio and on into Switzerland.

What is "Norway feeling" for you and why should everyone have been to Norway at least once? The fjords and the mountains surrounding them. And then stop for local strawberries. You should go because photos don't do it justice. Even the ones in CURVES Magazine.

Do Norwegians have a different approach to driving than people in other countries? Hmmm, good question. They are more careful than Southern Europeans, I guess. But they are better on bends than the average driver from Germany, Denmark, etc. And we do drive a lot of electric cars.

Let's forget about cars for a moment: where is the most beautiful place in Norway for you? Lots of places on the route I described: Tromsø to Trondheim. Senja Island is one of them.

Electric drive or combustion engine? I'm a big fan of electric drive. For everyday use. And I think we'll see some pretty cool electric race cars soon. For both, we need to make the infrastructure work. The car performance is already great.

Do you prefer to travel with a passenger or on your own? On my own, ha ha. Sounds strange, but I enjoy the quiet and the space to think.

And what's on the stereo? A podcast for the long drives when you need to get somewhere. Some rock classics for the fun drives. But also just quietness. Nothing on the radio. Enjoying the car and the natural surroundings.

BAC KST AGE

Kaum mit der letzten CURVES-Ausgabe aus Island zurückgekehrt, setzen wir unseren Flirt mit dem hohen Norden fort. Bilder aus Norwegen haben uns schon lange im Schlaf verfolgt, genau wie die Ahnung, dass die Landschaft an der Westküste Skandinaviens nicht nur ungeheuer fotogen sein muss, sondern ganz bestimmt auch Stoff für eine epische Reise bietet: im CURVES-Groove von jenseits des Polarkreises bis nach Süden an die Skagerrak-Küste. Dazwischen liegen Straßen, die entweder entlang des Meeres führen, oder sich durch die Inlandsgebirge schlagen. Und weil Norwegen von so ruppiger Natur geprägt ist, von Fjorden, Seen, Inseln und Gebirgszügen, haben beide Routen enorme Hindernisse zu überwinden: Wasser, Berge, Täler. Es sind diese natürlichen Herausforderungen an eine Route, die eine Reise für uns spannend und vielfältig machen: über Passstraßen die Berge erklimmen, einem Verlauf folgen, der wild und verwegen ist, großartige Landschaften genießen.

Und man kann es nicht anders sagen: Norwegen hat all unsere Erwartungen weit übertroffen. Man muss die Majestät der Fjorde mit eigenen Augen gesehen haben, um sie zu fühlen. Man muss die derbe, raue Welt am Polarkreis erlebt haben, um sie zu verstehen. Man muss Teil der langen Tage des Sommers im Norden gewesen sein, um ihren trägen Puls in den Adern zu haben. Man muss die unaufhörliche Weite des Lands durchstreift haben, um sie auf seiner inneren Landkarte abbilden

Although our feet have hardly touched the ground since returning from Iceland with the last issue of CURVES, we are continuing our flirtation with the far north. Images from Norway have been haunting our dreams for a long time, as has the feeling that the landscape of the west coast of Scandinavia must not only be tremendously photogenic, but also offers plenty of material for an epic journey: get into the CURVES groove from beyond the Arctic Circle to south to the Skagerrak coast.

In between are roads that either run along the sea or cut through the mountains of the interior. Because Norway is characterized by such rugged nature, with fjords, lakes, islands and mountain ranges, both routes have enormous obstacles to overcome: water, mountains, valleys.

It is these natural challenges along the way that make a trip so exciting and varied for us: climbing the mountains over mountain passes, following a route that is wild and daring, enjoying fabulous landscapes. There is no denying that Norway far exceeded all our expectations. You have to see the majesty of the fjords with your own eyes to feel it. You have to experience the raw, harsh world of the Arctic Circle to really understand it. You have to have lived through the long days of northern summer to feel their sluggish pulse in your veins. You have to have covered the endless expanse of the country to be able to make sense of it on your own internal map

zu können – und die ist nach einer Reise durch Norwegen schlagartig viel größer. Wir sind mit derselben Leidenschaft in diese Reise gestartet wie wir es immer tun, voller Ungeduld und Vorfreude und voller Pläne. Sind über die von Inseln und Meeresarmen geprägte Küste jenseits des Polarkreises gefahren, mit weit offenen Augen und hellwachen Sinnen. Gebannt, gespannt, hingerissen. Und dann hat uns Norwegen mit jedem zurückgelegten Kilometer mehr und mehr eingeholt. Die unerträgliche Weite dieses Landes ... Fahren in Norwegen, das fühlt sich an, wie die Zeit selbst: Manchmal berstend vor Leben, gefüllt mit Ereignissen – und dann ist da wieder nur eine in Zeitlupe ablaufende Heavy Rotation von Farben, Landschaften, Natur. All das in stetiger Wiederholung, nur aufgebrochen durch Veränderung in kleinen Nuancen. Slow-Motion-Sightseeing haben wir es genannt, irgendwann, als aus Frust und Resignation plötzlich ein Ankommen wurde. Das stille Zufriedensein mit dem Rhythmus einer Reise, die sich in ergebene Gelassenheit wandelt und schließlich zum Teil der Landschaft wird.

Man kann diesen vielen Kilometern nicht sein Tempo aufzwingen, man muss Geduld haben. Und fährt mit weit aufgestellten Antennen, deren Empfindlichkeit immer höher geregelt wird, die immer feiner empfangen. Sensibel für die ungeheure Schönheit Norwegens im Großen wie im Detail. Der famose Porsche Macan GTS, in dem wir unterwegs sein durften, hat sich dieser stillen Gangart überraschend gut angepasst. Er ist ein hitziges Eisen, ein Feuerkopf – aber hier wurde er zum feinen Muli für Mensch und Material. Wir werden ihn vermissen. Und sagen Danke, an Porsche, dass dieser wunderbare Reisegenosse am Ausgangspunkt der Reise auf uns gewartet hat und uns dann bis ans Ende der Fahrt begleiten durfte. Er ist viele Tage lang unser Zuhause gewesen. Das verbindet. Aber natürlich haben wir auf dem langen Weg nach Süden auch darüber diskutiert, welches Auto wir unseren Lesern als eine Empfehlung mitgeben würden: Was ist unser Traumauto auf dieser Fahrt? – Über die Antwort haben wir lange gebrütet und dann zu einer ganz einfachen Antwort gefunden: Porsche 356 A, 44 PS. Er wäre ein Auto wie das Land, knorrig und einfach und abenteuerlich. Sein Tempo käme dem der Straße kongenial entgegen – und auch dem, was in Norwegen erlaubt ist. Eilig haben sollte man es hier nicht, denn die Polizei mag das nicht. Selbst geringe Geschwindigkeitsübertretungen sind Anlass für drakonische Strafen, dieses CURVES empfiehlt also ganz klar: Take your time! Dann ist eine Entdeckung auch nicht weit: Auf dem langen Weg kommt man die ganze Zeit an. Strandet im gemächlichen Rhythmus der Dörfer und Höfe, erlebt die zurückhaltend-rustikale Freundlichkeit der Menschen, wird zum routinierten Fährmann, legt sich die unterkühlte Schweigsamkeit des Nordens zu. Und vielleicht hat man dann auch genug Zeit, um sich der norwegischen Küche zu widmen. Essen, das hat sich unterwegs zum heimlichen Hobby der CURVES-Macher entwickelt, und jetzt, während wir die Erinnerungen der

because everything suddenly seems so much bigger after a journey through Norway. We started this journey with our customary passion, full of impatience and anticipation and with our heads packed with plans. We have driven across a coast studded with islands and inlets beyond the Arctic Circle, with wide-open eyes and heightened senses, enthralled, excited, enraptured. We found that Norway wormed its way into our senses more and more with every kilometer we traveled. The unbearable vastness of this country... Driving in Norway feels like time itself: sometimes bursting with life and filled with incident – and then again there's just a slow-motion heavy rotation of color, landscape and nature. All of this is constantly repeated, only broken up by small variations in nuance. We called it slow-motion sightseeing at some point when, in a fug of frustration and resignation, we suddenly found we had arrived at our destination. The quiet contentment with the rhythm of a journey transforms itself into serene surrender as you finally become part of the landscape. You can't impose your own pace on distances of so many kilometers and need to be patient. You also need to drive with all your receptors turned up to maximum and fine-tuned to your surroundings to really appreciate the immense beauty of Norway, both large and small.

The famous Porsche Macan GTS we were allowed to use for our travels adapted surprisingly well to this quiet pace. Although it is generally a fiery hot-head, here it proved itself the ultimate packhorse for us and our equipment. We will miss it. We'd like to say thank you to Porsche for arranging for this wonderful travel companion to await us at the start of our journey and to accompany us right to the end. It was our home for many days. That forges a sense of connection. Of course on the long journey south we also discussed which car we would recommend to our readers: what would be our dream car on this trip? – We pondered the answer for a long time and then came up with a very simple answer: the Porsche 356 A, 44 hp.

This would be a car like the country itself: gnarly, uncomplicated and adventurous. Its speed would be the ideal match for the road – and also for Norway's speed limits. You need to slow down here, because the police don't like speed freaks. Even minor speed violations are grounds for draconian penalties, so CURVES definitely advises you to take your time! There are constantly new discoveries just around the corner: time is the key on this long journey. Lose yourself in the leisurely rhythm of the villages and farms, experience the reserved, rustic friendliness of the people, become an experienced ferry user, and embrace the cool reticence of the north. Maybe then you will have enough time to devote to Norwegian cuisine. Eating has become the CURVES creators' secret hobby along the way, and now, as we review our memories of the Norway trip, we get the unsatisfactory feeling

Norwegen-Reise Revue passieren lassen, haben wir das unbefriedigende Gefühl, diesen Aspekt des Reisens in Norwegen vernachlässigt zu haben. Vielleicht werden wir ja einfach noch einmal fahren, um genauer hinzusehen? Oder Sie tun uns den Gefallen und vertreten uns auf ihrer kommenden norwegischen Entdeckungsreise in den Restaurants und Stuben? Wenn bei Ihnen etwas Probierfreude und ein Faible für handfest-ländliche Zutaten hinzukommt, steht ja selbst einem Ausflug in die rustikalen Winkel der norwegischen Küche nichts entgegen: Geräucherter und gekochter Schafskopf, aus dem in manchen Fällen sogar noch das mitgegarte Hirn gelöffelt werden kann, dürfte dabei die Messlatte recht hoch legen. Schwache Gemüter sollten sich also besser über gekochtes Hammelfleisch mit Kohl – das sogenannte Fårikål – langsam an solche Spezialitäten herantasten. Oder besser gleich bei unverfänglichem Rentiersteak und schmackhafter Fischsuppe bleiben. Und am Ende trifft man sich schließlich versöhnlich beim Preiselbeeren-Eischnee, der „Trollkrem". In Norwegen. Zwischen Meer und Berg.

Wir denken auf jeden Fall immer noch an den mürbe und mild schmeckenden Kabeljau im Hafen von Ålesund, der sich in einer hellen Soße zwischen Bergen aus Knoblauch-Kartoffelstampf so wohl gefühlt hat, und würden ihn gern einmal wiedersehen. Auch das Standardessen der unzähligen Fährfahrten hat sich bei uns zu einem halb belächelten, halb schmerzhaft vermissten Insider-Element etabliert: Hot Dogs. Groß oder klein, prall und schmackhaft oder weich und einsilbig, knackig mit Röstzwiebeln oder lasch und pur. Ein Hot Dog ging immer. Ganz im Gegensatz zu einem Glas Bier oder Wein zum Abendessen. Als Mannschaft mit Münchner Wurzeln sind wir von der 13-Euro-Maß der Oktoberfest-Wiesn ganz bestimmt nicht verhätschelt, aber die 15 Euro für eine Halbe in Norwegen haben uns dann doch verblüfft …

Vielleicht lesen Sie es zwischen den Zeilen heraus: Norwegen hat uns zwar restlos, aber nicht reibungslos begeistert. Die lange Fahrt vom Nordkap herunter bis an die Nordsee war immer wieder eine wahre Herausforderung. Man muss sich Norwegen tatsächlich erarbeiten, geschenkt wird einem hier nichts. Kein einziger Kilometer, keine Abkürzung, keine Bonuspunkte, kein Anfänger-Rabatt. Aber gerade deshalb sind wir am Ende dieser Fahrt so angetan – weil Norwegen unfassbar echt ist. Für Fortgeschrittene. Für Rolling Stones. Für Reisende mit Sitzfleisch. Und immer dann, wenn man meint, nicht mehr zu können, belohnt einen die überwältigende Schönheit Norwegens. Fahren mit allen Sinnen. Für die Einsteiger ins CURVES-Lebensgefühl haben wir natürlich trotzdem einen Vorschlag: Nehmen Sie sich einfach nur die Lofoten vor. Oder das Abenteuer südlich von Kristiansund: Die Atlantikstraße, den Trollstigen hinauf, bis zum Geirangerfjord. Oder das Land zwischen Sognefjord, Hardangerfjord und Lysefjord. Und wir wissen jetzt schon eines: Sie werden wiederkommen. Denn Norwegen geht unter die Haut.

that we neglected this aspect somewhat as we traveled around Norway. Maybe we'll just go back again for a closer look? Or maybe you'd do us a favor and take our place in the restaurants and dining rooms on your upcoming Norwegian voyage of discovery? If you have a taste for experimentation and a soft spot for solid, rural ingredients, there's nothing to stop you from taking a trip to the more rustic corners of Norwegian cuisine: smoked and cooked sheep's head, from which in some cases even the cooked brain can be spooned out probably sets the bar quite high. Weaker constitutions should therefore take a more round-about approach to such specialties via boiled mutton with cabbage – known as fårikål. Or better yet, stick to harmless reindeer steak and tasty fish soup. And the perfect end to any meal? Cranberry with whipped egg whites, known as "Trollkrem" in Norway. Somewhere between the mountains and the sea.

We certainly still have fond memories of the tender and mild-tasting cod in the port of Ålesund, which tasted so good in a light sauce between mountains of garlic and mashed potatoes, and we would love to experience it again. The standard meal on our countless ferry rides has also established itself as an insider joke that we laugh about, but still miss dreadfully: hot dogs. Large or small, plump and tasty or soft and simple, crunchy with fried onions or limp and pure. A hot dog was always just what the doctor ordered. Quite the opposite applied to a glass of beer or wine with dinner. As a team with roots in Munich, we are quite accustomed to paying 13 euros for a liter of beer in the Oktoberfest tents, but 15 euros for half a liter in Norway took the biscuit…

Perhaps you can read between the lines: we found Norway completely inspiring but not exactly easy. Every part of the long journey from the North Cape down to the North Sea was a real challenge. You really have to work your way through Norway, nothing is served up to you on a plate here. Not a single kilometer, no shortcuts, no bonus points, no beginner's discount. But that's exactly why we were so impressed at the end of this trip – because Norway is incredibly real. For experienced adventurers. For restless types. For sedentary travelers. Whenever you think you can't do it anymore, Norway's overwhelming beauty will reward you. Driving with all your senses.

Of course, we have a suggestion for those new to the CURVES attitude to life: just take a tour of the Lofoten Islands. Or try the adventure south of Kristiansund: the Atlantic Road up the Trollstigen to the Geirangerfjord. Or the countryside between the Sognefjord, Hardangerfjord and Lysefjord. There's one thing for certain: you'll be back. Because Norway gets under your skin.

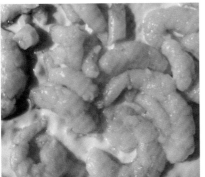

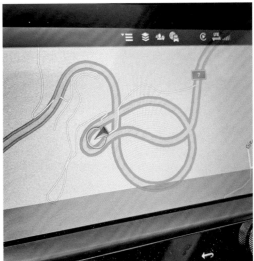

DANK AN / THANKS TO
Bastian Schramm, Maximilian Ramisch, Michael Daiminger, Ben Winter, Nadja Kneissler, Axel Gerber, Hanno Vienken, Michael Dorn, Michaela Bogner

SPECIAL FX / SPECIAL FX
AOT Travel - Christian Preiherr, Roar Strande of Lofoten Flyklubb, Johannes og Elin, Thorstein Klingenberg, David Jensen, Morten, Aksel Lund Svindal, Knut Markeggard, Kjetil Føyen, Christian Caspersen, Holger Greim & the Porsche Center Tromsø Team.

CURVES TRAVEL AGENT:

AOT Travel • info@aottravel.de • Tel. +49 89 12 24 800

ROUTE AS GPX FILE:

Porsche Macan GTS
Kraftstoffverbrauch kombiniert in l/100 km: 9,9 (NEFZ), 11,7-11,3 (WLTP);
CO2-Emission in g/km kombiniert: 225 (NEFZ), 265-255 (WLTP); Stand 07/2022

Fuel consumption combined in l/100km: 9,9 (NEDC), 11,7-11,3 (WLTP);
CO2-emissions combined in g/km: 225 (NEDC), 265-255 (WLTP); as of 07/2022

Porsche 911 Carrera GTS
Kraftstoffverbrauch kombiniert in l/100 km: 10,3-9,7 (NEFZ), 11,4-10,4 (WLTP);
CO2-Emission in g/km kombiniert: 234-221 (NEFZ), 258-236 (WLTP); Stand 07/2022

Fuel consumption combined in l/100km: 10,3-9,7 (NEDC), 11,4-10,4 (WLTP);
CO2-emissions combined in g/km: 234-221 (NEDC), 258-236 (WLTP); as of 07/2022

IMPRESSUM / IMPRINT

HERAUSGEBER/
PUBLISHER: CURVES MAGAZIN
THIERSCHSTRASSE 25
D-80538 MÜNCHEN

VERANTWORTLICH FÜR
DEN HERAUSGEBER/
RESPONSIBLE FOR
PUBLICATION:
STEFAN BOGNER

KONZEPT/CONCEPT:
STEFAN BOGNER
THIERSCHSTRASSE 25
D-80538 MÜNCHEN
SB@CURVES-MAGAZIN.COM

DELIUS KLASING
CORPORATE PUBLISHING
SIEKERWALL 21
D-33602 BIELEFELD

REDAKTION/
EDITORIAL CONTENT:
STEFAN BOGNER
BEN WINTER

ART DIRECTION, LAYOUT,
FOTOS/ART DIRECTION,
LAYOUT, PHOTOS:
STEFAN BOGNER

MAKING OF PHOTOS:
MICHAEL DAIMINGER

TEXT/TEXT: BEN WINTER
TEXT INTRO/TEXT INTRO:
BEN WINTER

MOTIVAUSARBEITUNG
LITHOGRAPHIE/SATZ/

POST-PRODUCTION,
LITHOGRAPHY/SETTING:
MICHAEL DORN

KARTENMATERIAL/MAP
MATERIAL: MAIRDUMONT,
OSTFILDERN

ÜBERSETZUNG/TRANSLATION
JAMES O'NEILL

PRODUKTIONSLEITUNG/
PRODUCTION MANAGEMENT:
AXEL GERBER

DRUCK/PRINT:
KUNST- UND WERBEDRUCK
BAD OEYNHAUSEN

1. AUFLAGE/1ST EDITION:
ISBN: 978-3-667-11679-6

AUSGEZEICHNET MIT / AWARDED WITH
**DDC GOLD - DEUTSCHER DESIGNER CLUB E.V. FÜR GUTE GESTALTUNG // IF COMMUNICATION DESIGN AWARD
BEST OF CORPORATE PUBLISHING // ADC BRONZE // RED DOT BEST OF THE BEST & D&AD // NOMINIERT FÜR
DEN DEUTSCHEN DESIGNPREIS // WINNER AUTOMOTIVE BRAND CONTEST // GOOD DESIGN AWARD**

CURVES AUSGABEN / OTHER ISSUES OF CURVES

Mountain roads look best from above.

Get there faster. Get there in comfort.
With Lufthansa.

Time for New Horizons.

Lufthansa
Say yes to the world

**Wie Liebe.
Auf den ersten Blick.
Bei jedem Blick.**

More of what you love. Die 911 GTS Modelle.

Mehr unter www.porsche.de/911GTS